INDIANA
BEACH

INDIANA BEACH

BEACH

• A Fun-Filled History •

W.C. MADDEN

THE
History
PRESS

Published by The History Press
Charleston, SC 29403
www.historypress.net

Copyright © 2014 by W.C. Madden
All rights reserved

Cover photos courtesy of Indiana Beach and Ruth Spackman Davis.
All internal images are courtesy of Indiana Beach unless otherwise noted.

First published 2014

Manufactured in the United States

ISBN 978.1.62619.297.3

Library of Congress CIP data applied for.

CONTENTS

ACKNOWLEDGEMENTS

When I was contacted by The History Press to write this book, I already had plans to write it six months before but I hadn't started on the project, so their timing was perfect. However, I had other things on my plate, so I had to put it to the side until November 2013, and the deadline was the end of the year. This didn't deter me, and I dedicated myself to finishing it on time, thanks to the help of some people like the Spackman family. Unfortunately, the elder Tom Spackman suffered a stroke in early November and passed away before I could speak with him. However, his children spoke for him and granted me interviews. They also helped me gather photos for the book.

Thanks to all the people who gave me interviews for this book. They were very helpful in my understanding of the park and what it means to people.

I would like to thank the White County Historical Society and the Monticello-Union Township Library for the vertical files they kept on Indiana Beach. Those files are helpful to a researcher like me and saved me time in the process. I would also like to thank the staff of the White County Records Department for digging through their old files and providing me some research information.

Thanks to Dorothy Salvo Davis for providing the information on the paranormal visit to Indiana Beach. And I appreciate the research help I received from Sabrina Gravely.

I would be remiss if I didn't thank my wife for helping me finish this book by doing things I would normally help her with at Christmastime. She also helped by editing my work before it was sent to the publisher.

INTRODUCTION

While many businesses begin in a basement or a garage, Indiana Beach started simply as a place to swim or rent a rowboat. Then it became a place where people could also dance and listen to orchestras. Then permanent rides were added, and it became like a carnival with a beach and a ballroom. Then roller coasters were built, and it became what it is today, a medium-sized amusement and water park with slides, rides, a zip line and much more.

What began as a place owned by an entrepreneur that was handed down to his son and eventually run by his family is now owned by a corporation and run by more than one thousand employees. What began as Ideal Beach, drawing a few thousand people a summer, is now Indiana Beach and draws nearly one million people a year.

This book captures the eighty-eight-year history of this Midwest amusement park.

Chapter 1

IDEAL BEACH

1920s

The roots of Indiana Beach date back to 1921, when construction began on the Norway Dam on the Tippecanoe River. When construction was completed in June 1923, Shafer Lake was formed. This allowed for the development of property surrounding the lake for summer cottages and homes to enjoy lake activities, like swimming, boating and fishing.

Earl W. Spackman, a distributor for the Ideal Furnace Company in Indianapolis, wanted a place for his family to get away from the big city. He wanted to be by the water. When he lived in Detroit, he owned a boat that he would use on the Detroit River. Earl heard about a new development on a lake two hours north of the state capital. He came to Monticello and was shown the new development by Thomas W. O'Connor, the former mayor of the little city. The lots along the lake had seventy-five feet of lakefront. He picked out a lot on the west side of Shafer Lake in the Untalulti Cottage Addition about two miles from the city. *Untalulti* is an Indian word meaning "lodge by the lake." Spackman had a cottage constructed and started taking his family to the lake during the summer for some relaxation.

The unusual thing about the property was that there were no outhouses. Everything was modern, with indoor plumbing. Also, people would stop at his place and ask him if there was any place for swimming on the lake. There was none. This gave Earl an idea. The bank that had started the development got into financial trouble and could no longer keep its building promises.

Rowboats were one of the first attractions at Ideal Beach. In the background of this postcard are the toboggan, bathhouse and first pier.

Earl could lease some property from the bank in order to help it out, but he lacked the funds. He asked his company if it would lease some land and he'd make a beach out of it. His company obliged with one condition: name the beach after the company. He agreed to name it Ideal Beach. That was the beginning of what would eventually become Indiana Beach.

When the water was lowered in Shafer Lake in September 1925 to fill Freeman Lake, where Oakdale Dam had been constructed, Earl took the occasion to have gravel brought in by mule teams to lay down a base for his beach on top of the mud that was once a cornfield. The gravel was spread manually, using shovels and two-by-four pieces of wood. Then he brought in tons of sand for the beach. When the lake filled back up, he had his man-made beach. Next, he constructed a bathhouse, a pier, a picnic pavilion and a small refreshment stand. Earl spent about $5,000 (about $64,000 today) on the improvements. For the rest of the decade, Ideal Beach was used for swimming and rowing boats.

When everything was ready, Spackman opened Ideal Beach on June 16, 1926, a Wednesday. "We had ten row boats, a pop stand, and a place to change your clothes," said Tom Spackman, who worked at the refreshment stand at the time, on the television show *Across Indiana*. He was twelve years old at the time. A pavilion was also constructed for picnics and a pier for fishing. The new beach charged $0.10 (about $1.32 today) to use

The water wheel pictured in this postcard was first introduced in 1927 at Ideal Beach.

the beach (children under six were free). The bathhouse had forty private rooms and charged $0.15 for children under twelve, $0.25 for teens and $0.40 for adults. Everyone who came to the beach was charged $0.10 if they came in their own bathing suits. No one was permitted to change clothes in their cars or toilets.

Earl hired William Russow to manage the beach. The beach employed five people, including his son. The refreshment stand offered hot dogs, drinks and other items to the hungry bathers after they swam or rowed boats.

In late June, Earl became the owner of eighty-six lots in the Untalulti addition. By the end of the summer, he had sold sixty-two lots. Also opening in 1926 was the Hillcrest Dance Pavilion on Shafer Lake.

The weather in the summer of 1926 was not very favorable, so people didn't flock to Ideal Beach as Earl had hoped. So he sold his beach to George Spurlock in the fall, according to the *Monticello Evening Journal*.

Spurlock took Earl's idea and expanded on it. In the off-season, he built a hotel and cottages for guests. The hotel had seven rooms for employees, twenty rooms for guests and a large dining room capable of seating thirty people. He also had a dozen cottages constructed. To make the beach more attractive and exciting, he had a toboggan ride built, a water wheel placed in the water and a diving platform constructed on the pier. People could slide down the thirty-foot toboggan and make a big splash in Shafer Lake.

Spurlock opened the beach on May 27, 1927, a Friday, the day before Decoration Day (now called Memorial Day). The charge to stay in the hotel

Swimmers enjoy Ideal Beach in this postcard. The toboggan slide is in the background, and people had fun sliding down it.

was three dollars a day (about forty dollars today) or eighteen dollars a week. The price included board, room and a rowboat. A chicken dinner would be served every day in the dining room. Apparently, things didn't work out for Spurlock, and he sold the beach back to Earl.

In 1928, Earl added another attraction to Ideal Beach. He started taking people around Shafer Lake in a passenger boat. The trip took more than an hour and ran every hour and a half. The fare was a quarter. Tom also began selling fireworks at the refreshment stand. By this time, Tom was attending Shortridge High School in Indianapolis.

The following year, the Monon Railroad offered round-trip weekend excursions from Indianapolis and Chicago. The Monon station in Monticello was the closest to the beach, only about five miles away. On a nice summer day, Ideal Beach drew three to four hundred bathers, and all rowboats would be rented. Times were good.

By 1929, Earl had sold off all the lots he had originally leased near the beach. He thought it would take him much longer, but other people saw the opportunity to purchase property to build cottages on the lake. He also increased the size of the bathhouse. The stock market crashed in October, and real estate sales slowed tremendously after that for quite a while, so Earl prospered from the sales in the nick of time.

Earl also saw the popularity of the Hillcrest Dance Pavilion located across the lake, so he decided to build one himself to accommodate four hundred couples at one time. Construction was started in late 1929.

1930s

Further expansion of Ideal Beach occurred during the decade that resulted in the number of employees increasing to thirty-five people. That number remained steady throughout the decade, as further expansion of the facility was not an option with the Great Depression sweeping across the nation. However, the hard times didn't seem to affect Ideal Beach as adversely as they did some other businesses, which shut their doors.

Earl rushed construction in the spring of 1930 to get the new dance hall, called Ideal Beach Casino, ready by May 30. It was not to be. Just hours after construction was completed on the day the beautiful dance hall was to open, a fire broke out at 2:30 a.m. Employee Rann Horning was awakened by the crackling fire and sounded the fire alarm. Frantic calls were made to the Monticello Fire Department, but the department failed to respond because Ideal Beach was outside its jurisdiction. Even if it had responded, it wouldn't have been able to put the fire out. The structure was made of wood and was completely razed by the fire. Electrical workers had been working at the structure up to two hours before the fire, but officials were uncertain of the cause of the blaze.

Communication was not nearly as good in those days, so many people had not heard about the fire. Couples flocked to Ideal Beach by the thousands only to find a pile of ashes instead of a dance hall. Patrons were disappointed by the fire, but not nearly as much as the owner.

The blaze also claimed the refreshment pavilion and decimated the fleet of eighteen rowboats. The entire contents in the dance hall were destroyed as well, including a grand piano, a popcorn popper, a peanut machine, two automatic ticket machines and a host of other supplies. The loss was estimated at $20,000, but only $8,000 was covered by the insurance that Earl had purchased with W.N. Scott Insurance.

The bathhouse was spared by the fire, as was the hotel. That was a blessing since the bathhouse contained one hundred dressing rooms, eight hundred bathing suits, 2,200 towels and 1,200 baskets for rent.

A couple days later, the undaunted Earl announced plans to build another dance hall. An open-air dance hall with a canopy would be used until a permanent structure could be built. To finance the project, he sold coupon books to be used at Ideal Beach. He hoped to open the dance pavilion by July 4. The fire also delayed the opening of the beach until June 15, a Sunday.

Besides a new casino, work was progressing on three new cottages. These were large cottages that would rent for twenty-five dollars a week. One would be reserved for the orchestra playing in the casino.

Workers worked feverishly and completed the new casino early. It opened on Saturday night, June 28, a week ahead of schedule. The new dance floor measured sixty feet by eighty feet and was smaller than the original facility that had burned down. Earl did that in order to build it more quickly. He called the casino "the most ambitious project since the construction of the hydro-electric dams" in the *Monticello Herald*.

The '30s was the big band era, and the Chic Meyers Orchestra was the first band to perform at the casino and played the whole first summer. Dances were held nightly after Ideal Beach opened for the season. Because of the Depression, Earl kept prices down for dancing by not hiring named bands until the economy improved. The dance casino started the decade with local and regional bands like the Monticello Boys' Band, St. Louis Blue Blowers, New Orleans Ramblers, Frosty Graham and His Bandoliers, Bernie Young Orchestra, Harry Jones and His Orchestra, Dick Sheldon and His Orchestra, Jimmy Raschel and His New Orleans Ramblers, Karl Lane and His Campus Boys from the University of Illinois, Ralph Bennett and His Lucky Strike Orchestra, Byron Dunbar and his eleven radio and recording artists, Al Roderick and His Orchestra and America's youngest blues singer, nine-year-old Barbara Graham. Many of the bands found it convenient to stop at Ideal Beach on their way from Indianapolis to Chicago.

In 1934, the economy started to improve, so Earl increased the size of the dance casino and went after some nationwide bands. He began with Johnny "Skinny" Hamp and His Kentucky Serenaders; McKinney's Cotton Pickers, a famous African American band at the time; Johnny Davis and

Cars could park close to the Ideal Beach Casino, as shown in this 1939 photo. *Courtesy Ruth Spackman Davis.*

His Orchestra, an NBC coast-to-coast band; Don Pablo Orchestra and the 14 Virginians; "Tweet" Hogan and His Orchestra; Karl Rich and His Orchestra; Joe Cappo and His Egyptian Serenaders; Dick Ward and His 14 Californians; and Lop Jarman, the world's greatest Euphonium player (a conical-bore, baritone-voiced brass instrument). The resort sometimes also featured a Battle of the Music Night by having two orchestras play the same night.

Bigger named orchestras started coming in 1936 with the likes of "Tiny" Hill and His Band. Tiny was actually Harry Lawrence Hill, who weighed 365 pounds and was dubbed "America's biggest band leader." Probably the biggest turnout for the year was 2,400 paid admissions to see Dick Cisne and his twelve-piece band. There was not enough parking for the event, although the parking lot could hold 2,800 cars. Parking was free.

Then, in 1937, Eddie Cantor and His Orchestra came in May. Cantor was a singer, actor and radio personality. He had performed in the Ziegfield Follies for many years in New York City. Then Duke Ellington and His Orchestra came to play later that year. The beach sold advance tickets for $0.99 each or $1.20 (about $20.00 today) at the door. Ellington was an African American who became famous in the Roaring Twenties playing at the Cotton Club in Harlem. He started recording songs and took his orchestra around the country to perform. Ellington would go on to become very famous and earned a dozen Grammy awards. He was named to several music halls of fame and earned many other honors. Andy Hansen and his fifteen-piece orchestra and Carl Noble and His Orchestra also came to play to close out the decade. Al Katz and His Kittens came direct from the Arcadia Ballroom in New York City to perform on July 29. The Kittens were female singers who were first introduced into dance bands in the early 1930s. Several bands came back to play more than once in the '30s.

Ideal Beach also offered special nights for the dances to attract people on nights other than the weekend. The resort offered Waltz Night, Collegiate Night, Penny Night, Square Dancing Night, etc. Dances in the '30s usually began in April before Easter and continued on Sunday nights—later Saturday nights—until the end of May. Then the resort would be open daily up until Labor Day and dances were provided nightly and on Sunday afternoons. In 1930, bands continued twice a week until the end of the year. Earl also decided to keep the hotel open all winter for hunters. That never happened again.

At first, Spackman charged men fifty cents and women a quarter in the dance hall. On Sunday afternoons, he charged a dime. If a more expensive band was playing, he would charge couples about a dollar (about seventeen dollars today). Dance lessons cost two dollars for eight lessons. However, Sunday afternoons were a bargain, as dancers were charged only a penny for lessons. On Sunday nights, admission was a nickel or a penny per dance.

The dance casino was doubled in size to six thousand square feet in 1937 with the opening of an open-air dance floor that had a roll-back roof in case of inclement weather.

Of course, the dance hall was also available to rent for special events, like proms, meetings, conventions, etc. A style show extravaganza was held with models from Indianapolis helping out, and of course, it drew a lot of people. Seybolds Dry Goods Store of Logansport used the ballroom for a style show. Thirty models showed off the latest summer fashions.

Besides the big bands, Earl brought in special attractions to lure more people to Ideal Beach for other entertainment, as vaudeville acts were plentiful in those days. These were held during the afternoon and were free to customers. One of the vaudeville acts that summer of 1931 was a free five-act dog show on a Sunday in August. Another was the acclaimed singer Barbara Graham. A big minstrel show involving a troupe of actors singing, dancing and doing comic dialogue was also held.

Earl started the decade with the Great Pasha. The daredevil was buried under six feet of dirt just like a corpse and then resurrected two hours later, still alive. After that, he drove through Monticello blindfolded. The resort that day had a circus-like atmosphere as it brought in animals and served peanuts, Cracker Jacks and pink lemonade. Another daredevil who traveled to Ideal Beach was Hardini, an escape artist. Unfortunately, the escape artist was unable to get out of a box that he was nailed to, so he was quite embarrassed. However, he did get out of a straitjacket suspended forty feet in the air. He was followed by Sardini, a new escape artist. These escape artists tried to mimic the great Harry Houdini, who died in 1926.

On Fourth of July weekends, Ideal Beach presented boat races, parachute jumps and fireworks. Record crowds jammed the new dance hall. The park offered $1,000 in prize money for the boat races, which ran each day of the weekend. Earl provided two emergency boats to handle any accidents, as well as an ambulance on land if needed. The best place to view the fireworks show was from a boat in the lake. He also had temporary stands erected that held two thousand people to see the boat races and fireworks show. Free movies were shown on Monday nights.

Earl brought in concession stands and rides, including a merry-go-round and Ferris wheel. He also had a powerful amplifying system installed to broadcast music over the entire grounds. He even allowed local talent to sing on the microphone at times. In 1935, a new ride came to Ideal Beach in the form of a twenty-two-foot eight-passenger boat provided by Paul McGriff of West Lafayette.

Because of the hard times, Earl made swimming at the beach free to start the 1930s. Later when he did charge, he made Wednesdays Children's Day at Ideal Beach. Children got in free unless they wanted to change and check their clothes in the bathhouse, but the charge was reduced to five cents for that. Children's Day became very popular, and more than one thousand kids would show up on those days. Two lifeguards were on duty on these days.

Starting in 1933, an adult could get a season pass for $1.00, while the charge for a child was just $0.50. Earl charged children under age twelve

Some kids literally enjoyed hanging around Ideal Beach, as in this photo.

$0.05 to get in. He also charged a dime for a towel (about $1.75 today). A new policy was instituted for bathers in 1934. Since season and weekly tickets were being offered at greatly reduced prices, tickets were made non-transferable. The price of a season pass stayed the same, but a weekly pass was also offered. For a weekly pass, adults were charged $0.35 and children were charged $0.20. A one-day pass cost $0.10. The charge for the bathhouse and a towel was $0.15. Visitors could get a wool suit, towel and other extras for $0.35 more. A half hour on the toboggan cost $0.15.

Rumors were going around that Ideal Beach was not safe for bathers in 1934. However, the beach assured bathers that the water was safe, as it was always moving through Shafer Lake toward the dam.

More picnics were also being held at Ideal Beach. One of the largest picnics hosted four hundred employees from the R.B.M. Factory in

Tom Spackman brought in the Ferris wheel as one of the first permanent rides in 1947. *Courtesy Ruth Spackman Davis.*

Logansport. Camping also increased, including a troop of Boy Scouts who spent a week camping in their pup tents.

Besides the new dance hall, construction continued at Ideal Beach in the 1930s to make the facility bigger and better. A new bathhouse was built in 1932 to accommodate up to five thousand people. During the summer, Earl also built more cottages to provide more indoor housing for visitors. A new toboggan slide was constructed during 1934. Spackman also hired a man to build three billboards to advertise to motorists traveling along U.S. 24 and Indiana 39. He even went as far as buying the property where the signs were located so he wouldn't have to pay rent. He was a big believer in good, professional signs for his messages. The billboards included some eye-catching rides, the name and the directions. He also started advertising in

The Roof Garden was constructed in 1934 after Prohibition ended. Alcohol was served on one side, and nonalcoholic drinks were served on the other side.

Indianapolis and other city newspapers to bring Hoosiers from all over the state to his resort.

As a result of Prohibition coming to an end in 1933, Earl expanded the casino and built the Roof Garden in 1934. The ballroom started selling alcohol, and the Roof Garden served alcohol on one side and nonalcoholic beverages on the other. A beer cost $0.15 for a bottle or two for $0.25. A case of beer was $2.25 warm or $2.50 (about $44.00 today) cold. Below the Roof Garden were a jukebox and a refreshment stand where many of the Spackmans worked. "It was like a Dairy Queen," said Joy (Spackman) Boomershine Bailey. "We'd make everything there, like splits, sundaes…"

Outdoor lights were installed in 1934 to brighten the park at night. This also allowed people to take a dip at night. The large pier that was built in 1935 was destroyed over the winter by an ice jam in Shafer Lake, so Earl unveiled plans for a U-shaped steel and cement pier to be built.

A frozen custard stand opened in 1936. That was a welcome sight, as it was so hot that people slept outside or went swimming in the evenings to cool off. The heat wave began in late June and created a drought in Indiana as well. Temperatures rose as high as 112 in the state during a time that had no air conditioning.

The toboggan ride became a double ride where two people could ride in the car, but it went back to one to be safer. *Courtesy Ruth Spackman Davis.*

The swimming area was first enclosed in 1937 by a wooden promenade pier.

Earl and Tom Spackman traveled to Russell's Point, Ohio, in 1936 and purchased a speed boat that could reach thirty-five miles per hour on the water to give visitors a thrilling ride.

Another major change to the beach was a larger 12-foot-wide, 650-foot-long wooden promenade pier that was built around the bathing beach. The enclosed bathing area made it safer for swimmers; however, the water from Shafer Lake was still used. Also, the water toboggan slide was expanded and rebuilt with a double track in 1937.

A new roller-skating rink was built in 1939. The latest music was played while people skated around the rink. Diving towers were added to the beach that year and located outside the swimming area.

Earl showed his love and compassion for children by allowing kids from the Indiana Soldiers' and Sailors' Children's Home in Knightstown to come to the resort for free. The twenty-five children were brought to Monticello by eight veterans from the American Legion. The children ranged in age from pre-kindergarten to high school.

1940s

The decade was full of changes with the coming of a world war and the switch from just a resort to more of an amusement park. Perhaps an omen of things to come in the '40s occurred in June 1940. The bridge over Honey Creek collapsed, making it difficult for summer lake visitors to get to Ideal Beach from Monticello. People had to take a detour around the creek for twenty-two days, while county workers labored eleven hours a day, seven days a week, to get the bridge reopened by July 20.

At the beginning of the era, the Spackmans completely redecorated the ballroom, and some new booths were added as they continued bringing in top named bands to Ideal Beach. Bands started playing on the weekends in March and performed until Labor Day.

The first big named band was Glenn Miller Orchestra, rated number one by several nationwide polls and *Billboard Magazine*. Advance sales were held for the event, which attracted a packed house. The orchestra was first formed in 1938 and had seven Billboard hit records that year. Miller's was perhaps the most famous orchestra that played a one-night stand in the ballroom.

Another famous band was Benny Goodman and His Orchestra. Dubbed the "King of Swing," Goodman was acclaimed as the best jazz clarinetist ever by some polls. He went on to appear in several movies.

After the war began, Earl decided not to cut back on entertainment, so he opened the casino on March 8 for Sunday concerts until Decoration Day at the end of May. This was the earliest Ideal Beach had ever opened. He did raise prices a little, as he charged ladies thirty cents and men sixty cents, a nickel and dime increase, respectively. Earl also started providing special police protection for parking.

During the decade, many of the bands that had appeared in the '30s came back for encore performances. The ballroom changed the way it charged in 1941. Dancing would now be included in the price of admission. Every Tuesday night was set aside as Waltz Night, when every other dance would be a waltz and the other dances would be slower, sweeter music.

During the war, the park had a hard time getting meat, sugar and other food items that were in short supply, but Tom Spackman was able to find a supplier in Michigan City who helped: Russell Luchtman, who had food concessions at Washington Park.

After the war came to the United States on December 7, 1941, things changed at Ideal Beach. Many of the orchestras lost members to the war effort, and Earl cut back on named bands. Of course, some of the employees of Ideal Beach went off to war as well. However, Ideal Beach remained popular and would go on because people still needed a place to relax and amuse themselves. Not everyone was fighting in the war. The war did have an effect on the fireworks show because of blackouts by Civil Defense. However, a fireworks show was provided by the Illinois Fireworks Company on Labor Day 1942.

One of the most famous bands that played at Ideal Beach was Tommy Dorsey and His Famous Orchestra. Dorsey was known as the "Sentimental Gentleman of Swing" because of his smooth trombone playing. He wrote about a dozen songs, and his orchestra was in nine movies before his appearance at Ideal Beach.

Tommy Dorsey performed at Ideal Beach and then gave out autographed photos like this one. *Courtesy Ruth Spackman Davis.*

Stan Kenton and His Orchestra also came to Ideal Beach. During his lifetime, he recorded nearly one hundred albums and won several Grammy awards. The composer, pianist and arranger performed for five decades.

Other famous orchestras included Dick Jurgens and His Orchestra from Chicago. Jurgens was a swing music bandleader who had a couple hit songs before he played at Ideal Beach for a one-night stint. He joined the U.S. Marines in 1942 and directed theater shows for the troops during the World War II. After the war, he had a hit show on CBS Radio. Larry Clinton and His Orchestra played in 1941. The bandleader recorded a string of hits for Victor Records. When the war broke out, he joined the U.S. Army Air Corps as a pilot and flew in the Hump airlift from Calcutta to China. The Mary Marshall Orchestra, with Mary dubbed "America's Most Beautiful Bandleader," brought in a large crowd of nearly 1,200 people for an Easter performance. Barney Rapp and His New Englanders played at the casino once. Rapp recorded several albums under RCA Victor and Bluebird. Kise Clinton and His Orchestra performed once as well. Clinton's orchestra was short-lived but recorded 214 sides for RCA Victor and Bluebird. Les Brown and His Famous Band of Renown played for one night. Brown performed for six decades, from 1938 to 2001. The group had ten number-one hits and later made many television appearances. Eddie Howard, a new singing star and composer, and His Orchestra came for one night. The California singer had a couple number-one hits after he performed at Ideal Beach. Vaughn Monroe and His Orchestra also performed once at Ideal Beach. Besides being a bandleader, Monroe was an actor and radio personality. He has two stars on the Hollywood Walk of Fame. Charlie Spivak, "the man that plays the sweetest trumpet in the world," also came to play. Typical admission for these named bands was about twenty dollars in today's money.

Other groups that played at Ideal Beach included the Byron Dunbar Orchestra; Don Colburn and His Eleven Commanders; Val Grayson and His Orchestra; Dick Mills and His Orchestra; Fred Coyle and His Orchestra from Hamilton, Ohio; Mel Pester and His Orchestra from Omaha; Dick Mills and His Orchestra; Hank Messer's Band; "Sternie" Sternberg and His Orchestra with Carl Bean; Jack Kirk and His Orchestra with Georgia Lane; Warren Snively Orchestra; Bud Roderick and His Orchestra from the University of Illinois; Ben Bradley and His Orchestra; Joe Ziney and His Orchestra from Butler University; Larry Clinton and His Orchestra; Freddy Schloot and His Orchestra from Iowa University; Doc Lawson and His Orchestra; Ernie Englund and His Twelve-Piece Orchestra; Keith Bussert and His Orchestra; Stan Sterbenz and His Orchestra from Indiana University; Dave Holmes and His Eleven-Piece Orchestra; Don Hampden and His Orchestra; John Mac Bruce and His Twelve-Piece Orchestra; Dale Higgins and His Twelve-Piece Orchestra; Joe Sanders and His Nighthawks; Johnny Hall Orchestra; Bob Alexander Orchestra; Tony Pastor Orchestra; Wayne Carr Orchestra; Andy Imperial Orchestra; Johnny Bruce and His Twelve-Piece Orchestra featuring Ginny Denton; Eddie Roe and His Orchestra from Ohio's Miami University; Will Hauser and His Orchestra from Cincinnati; Don Ragon and His Orchestra along with Alice Raye and Keith Milheim; Billy Bishop and His Orchestra; Tex Beneke Orchestra; Jimmy Featherstone Orchestra; Bob Leighton and His Orchestra; Lee Angolo and His Orchestra from Pittsburgh; Tony Di Pardo Orchestra; Eddie O'Neal Orchestra; Sherman Haynes Orchestra; Eddy Haddad and His Orchestra; Ben Ribble and His Orchestra; Buddy Divito and His Orchestra; Ray Pearl and His Musical Gems; and Russ Carlyle and His Orchestra.

Gene Autry's pal Smiley Burnette came to Ideal Beach along with radio and movie personalities to open the new corral open-air arena that was constructed at the end of the midway in 1949.

Singers started coming near the end of the decade. The regular orchestra provided music for them. Bobby Beers and Joan Mowery, vocalists with

Passengers wait for the *Fairy Queen* to dock. The boat was owned and operated by V.W. Schumacher and first launched in 1941. *Courtesy Ruth Spackman Davis.*

Lawrence Welk and His Orchestra, performed. Mowery was one of Welk's champagne ladies. Welk became more famous when he had his own television show. Sharon Rogers and June Christy also came to sing at the resort. Christy went on to record many songs with Capitol Records.

Earl continued to add some new attractions in the '40s. The first was a one-hundred-passenger excursion boat called the *Fairy Queen*. The boat began operation at Ideal Beach on Decoration Day 1941. V.W. Schumacher owned and operated the sixteen-foot-wide and forty-six-foot-long boat. He provided hourly trips on Shafer Lake. The boat could also be rented for parties.

A bowling alley was added in 1941. Bantam bowling featured shorter lanes, twenty-eight feet long. After Labor Day weekend in 1941, new management took over the roller-skating rink and put in a new maple floor. The rink was heated too. It held a gala opening on November 8 and offered skating all night. The charge was thirty-five cents for ladies and forty cents for men. The rink was open every Saturday night from 8:00 p.m. to midnight. In December, skating moved to Sunday nights, 7:30 to 11:30 p.m., until the war started. Sometimes ladies' night was offered and ladies got in free, but they had to pay a five-cent tax. "People loved to roller skate," said Joy. She

People walked on dirt before the boardwalk like that at Atlantic City was installed. *Courtesy Ruth Spackman Davis.*

learned how to skate in the late 1940s and enjoyed the rink herself as a child. "My parents let me go roller skating there. I didn't have to work then."

A new miniature golf course opened between the Roof Garden and the beach in 1942. Shuffleboard courts were added too. Spackman advertised Ideal Beach as "Indiana's Most Complete Summer Resort."

Archery was the new attraction at Ideal Beach in 1944. Four new automatic bowling lanes were added that year too.

During the war, Earl would serve fresh water in cups like the trains used to carry. He would sell them for a penny to pay for the cup. This was at the water fountain under the Roof Garden.

Near the end of the conflict, Earl stepped down from the board of directors and turned the reins over to his son, Tom. The following year, Earl passed away from a heart attack while on vacation in Canada.

After Earl's passing, Tom took the resort in a new direction, as he changed the theme from merely a resort to more of an amusement park. "I saw trends changing," Tom later explained in the *Monticello Herald Journal*. He also saw Santa Claus Land open in Santa Claus, Indiana, in August 1946. That was the first theme park in the world.

Tom's first step was to add first permanent rides in 1947. He did so with a Ferris wheel, a merry-go-round and the Roll-o-Plane (later renamed the Bullet). The rides came from Washington Park in Michigan City and were

The *Daddy Wahoo* was an inboard speedboat that took passengers quickly around Shafer Lake, as shown in this postcard. *Courtesy Ruth Spackman Davis.*

run by a concessionaire at first until Tom bought them later. Rides were also offered on the *Daddy Wahoo*, a Chris Craft wooden hull inboard speedboat that was owned by Hugo Butler. The boat operated from a dock next to the ballroom. The fast boat thrilled riders as it zoomed around Shafer Lake.

Tom announced in May 1947 that he would open a California-type drive-in. Jimbo Drive-In would be adjacent to North West Shafer Drive. That year also saw a new beauty salon for the ladies open during the summer. A new wooden floor was installed at the roller-skating rink too. The following year, the Jimbo Drive-In was burglarized, according to the *Logansport Pharos-Tribune*. Twenty-four dollars in nickels and dimes was taken from the cash register. Six packs of gum were also missing. Entrance was gained by breaking a window.

A new improvement to the resort in 1948 was the free picnic grove that provided room for four hundred people to eat at picnic tables.

Special promotions continued to bring people to Ideal Beach. The big promotion for opening day of the beach in 1941 was Mike Kelly's spectacular ride through fire. He rode a standard bicycle down a narrow ramp higher than the new toboggan tower and crashed through a wall of flame with only a four-inch clearance on each side for the handlebars.

Tom continued to be a promoter like his father as he brought in a turtle named Churubusco in 1949 for people to come and see all summer. Also that year, he brought in the high-flying act of Torina & Eric for free performances nightly and on weekend afternoons. Captain Earl McDonald performed high fire dives on Labor Day weekend.

The first Antique Auto Show was held in 1949. Collectors brought their antique vehicles to Ideal Beach to show off their wheels. The show continued to grow for many years to come, and more than one hundred vehicles would make their presence known.

The beach was still the main reason people came to the resort in the '40s, so admission was kept reasonable—eleven cents for adults and five cents for children at the beginning of the decade and not rising much from there.

A new concrete pier was built around the bathing beach in 1945. Instead of lake water, fresh water was provided by a well. A few years later, the resort started advertising that its water was tested by the state board of health, as it was no longer fed by the flowing lake. The schools conducted swimming lessons at Ideal Beach and also had swim meets. Swimmers would race from one end of the enclosed swimming area to the other. The Monticello Jaycees hosted an AAU-sponsored swim meet in 1949 that ran for several years.

Tragedy almost struck when a bather was accidentally electrocuted on a diving platform in 1942. Charles Carter, eighteen, fell into the water

The diving boards were located outside the swimming area to prevent anyone hitting a swimmer when they dived. *Courtesy Ruth Spackman Davis.*

as a result. Fortunately, the Purdue University student was able to walk away unhurt.

Ideal Beach was not exempt from criminal activity. Vandals stole three metal signs in 1943. The resort offered a $100 reward for information leading to the arrest of the culprits. The Shafer Lake Welfare Association also offered a $25 reward. The signs read "and his Orchestra," "to nite" and "next Sunday."

In 1949, nine arrests were made at Ideal Beach of people who brought their own alcoholic beverages. The arrests were made by Special Deputy Sheriff J. Ralph Ridenour. Each individual ended up being fined twenty-five dollars and had to pay courts costs of thirty-seven dollars each. One offender was sent to juvenile court.

The resort advertised for college students to work there because local high school students went back to school in mid-August and the park was open for another two weeks after that.

1950s

Ideal Beach only lasted two years into the '50s. However, some significant events occurred during those two years.

During the winter of 1950, construction work began on a new hotel at Ideal Beach. Also, Tom decided to launch a large advertising campaign to attract visitors to his park. He put his money into fifty colorful billboards, newspaper ads, radio spots and forty thousand pieces of direct mail.

No big-name orchestras came to play during this time, but several good new orchestras came to the ballroom to perform, such as Larry Looney Orchestra, Bob Doran Orchestra from Purdue University, Bill Carnegie and His Orchestra, Toby Davidson and His Orchestra, Glen Gray and His Famous Casa Loma Orchestra, Will Helms and His Band, Al Cassidy Orchestra and Claude Thornbill and His Orchestra. Thornbill, a famous pianist, was best known for his recording of "Snowfall" in 1941. The Terre Haute native played for several famous orchestras before forming his own band in 1951. Besides music, other talent was brought in to entertain, including Ziggy, the Talent Clown Prince of good humor.

Promotions continued, and one of the best ever was in 1950. This promotion was a stunt. Paul David Abbott spent 1,686 hours or seventy-one days under water to protest hidden taxes and high excise taxes. The press called the World War II veteran the "Tax Sucker." His six- by ten-foot glass-enclosed structure was constructed of half-inch glass and cost about $3,000 to build. The room weighed about three thousand pounds and was equipped with fluorescent lights, an intercom system and a telephone. Furniture included a day bed, an easy chair, a table, a lamp, a radio, a smoking stand and an Indian rug. A small closet allowed him to go to the bathroom in private. His room was submerged into Lake Shafer with about six inches of water above it. Visitors could walk around it and talk with the service veteran if they wanted.

On Father's Day 1950, Abbott stood in front of news and newsreel crews to explain why he was protesting. The event was covered by radio, reporters and crews from NBC, Fox Universal, MGM News of the Day and others.

Larry Norris remembered seeing Abbott and thought he was let out of the glass enclosure at night when the park was closed. "You could toss coins on top of the glass," Norris said. Nearly $100 worth of coins was collected during the summer.

Abbott's stay under water ran from June 18 to August 27. During the span of his stay, about 150,000 visitors saw Abbott. Congress failed to take any action as a result of his protest, so he left the tank just before the park closed after Labor Day. The twenty-seven-year-old father returned to his family and three children.

Years later, Abbott was interviewed by the *Logansport Pharos-Tribune* and said this about his experience: "I wouldn't take a million dollars for my experience, and I wouldn't pay a dime to do it again."

The promotion brought in thousands of visitors just to see Abbott. For example, a chartered bus full of Chicago people came in July primarily to see him, and about 5,000 came to see him get out of his underwater "home." The "Man Living under Water" stunt led Ideal Beach to receive the promotion of the year award from the National Association of Amusement Parks, Pools and Beaches. Manager Tom Spackman received press inquiries from nearly every state in America. The promotion helped to boost the attendance to more than 200,000 for the season.

The new Beach House Hotel was ready by Memorial Day weekend. Each room was equipped with a private bath, radiant electric heating and air conditioning. By this time, Ideal Beach had forty-eight modern cottages as well for housing. The resort was beginning to be used more and more often for weddings and honeymoons because of the facilities and services it could provide.

The Beach House Hotel, as shown in this postcard, was first built in 1950.

On the beach, people watched outboard hydroplane races in 1950. Admission to Vantage Point to watch the races was sixty cents. Children under twelve were free.

To promote water safety, Ideal Beach brought in the Red Cross Chapter of White County in late July 1950 to teach swimming; nearly one hundred people were taught how to swim.

The largest picnic to come to Ideal Beach during this two-year period was held by the Fairfield Manufacturing Company of Lafayette. This Sunday event brought in more than one thousand people.

In 1951, a new sand filtration system was added to the sewage disposal system at the resort. The system was installed after Tom consulted with engineers regarding the most effective and inexpensive way of obtaining satisfactory disposal of water from septic tanks. The new sand bed had a capacity of over three thousand gallons of water per hour.

On November 1, 1951, Ideal Beach was renamed Indiana Beach. Tom also changed it from a place for swimming and dancing to more of an amusement park that included some swimming and dancing. The new name was chosen from a large selection of names because management felt it best expressed the nature of the vacation spot. "I wanted something more geographical, so people would know they had been away from home," Tom later said about the name change in the

The "Boats and Beach" sign jutted up from the entrance to the beach to show people where to enter. *Courtesy Ruth Spackman Davis.*

Monticello Herald Journal. He also gave it new advertising slogans: "Riviera of the Midwest" and "Playground of the Midwest." These continued to be used into the 1970s.

Chapter 2
INDIANA BEACH BEGINS

1950s

The name change brought about some confusion, so advertising in 1952 contained "formerly Ideal Beach." Besides the name change, the '50s marked the coming of rock-and-roll music to the resort and the decline of the big band era. The park also expanded with the addition of an island in Lake Shafer. A free ski show was also added to provide a different kind of entertainment to visitors. After a trip to Atlantic City in 1951, Tom Spackman decided that he would bring the boardwalk idea to Indiana Beach. In the off-season, employees built the boardwalk for guests. The new boardwalk also led from the beach to the new Kiddyland, where the rides for younger children were located.

The first big rock-and-roll star to come to Indiana Beach was the famous Bill Haley & His Comets. The group came to perform two forty-five-minute shows in 1957. His "Rock around the Clock" song made him famous that year, and later that summer, he became the first major American rock singer to tour Europe and his song was the first to sell one million copies in Britain and Germany. He was posthumously inducted into the Rock and Roll Hall of Fame in 1987.

The Kingston Trio made its first appearance in the Hoosier state at Indiana Beach on July 25. The three singers rocketed to fame with their hit "Tom Dooley." They received a Grammy for the recording that year. They earned another Grammy the following year. The trio has been inducted into three

This is what Ideal Beach looked like in the early 1950s. *Courtesy Ruth Spackman Davis.*

halls of fame: Grammy, Vocal Group and Hit Parade. It contributed to both the folk and pop music culture. "That was the biggest crowd we ever had up to that point in time," remembered Ruth Spackman Davis. "Everyone was standing and people couldn't see the stage, so Dad made everyone sit down on the floor, and they did." Then they could see the group perform.

The fabulous Fabian appeared for two shows at Indiana Beach. The teen idol first appeared on *American Bandstand* in 1958. He made his screen debut that year in *Hound Dog Man.* He was in more than thirty films and earned a star on the Hollywood Walk of Fame in 2000. Ruth Spackman Davis cherishes the autograph she has from the handsome star.

Another famous group that played was the Chordettes. The attractive female quartet hit the big time in 1954 with a number-one song, "Mr. Sandman." Their song "Lollipop" reached number two on the charts in 1958, and they had a dozen other hit singles.

Besides American bands, a Canadian group stopped by Indiana Beach. The Crew-Cuts had a dozen hits on the American charts and a number one, "Sh-Boom," before coming to the park.

Another group that came was the Four Freshmen. The group released a number of recordings and made several television and movie appearances. Its popularity dwindled some in the 1960s when British pop was on the rise.

The Hilltoppers performed in 1959. They became famous with the 1954 hit "Till Then."

In 1951, a new stage was built for small musical groups. It was attached to the Roof Garden and was called the Roof Garden Lounge. Probably the most famous performer in the lounge was Boots Randolph Quartet, best known for his 1963 saxophone hit "Yakety Sax." Other performers at the lounge in the 1950s included Jackie Stevens, Max Holland on his organ, Jack Stephens, Carol Lee and the Echos and Johnny Barr. And music even came to the boardwalk in the afternoons when Russ Stackhouse started playing his organ there. A Boardwalk Lounge also opened in the mid-1950s. The Gadabouts trio played there once.

Top-named bands continued to be brought to Indiana Beach. One of the biggest was Louis Armstrong's one-night performance in 1956. "Satchmo" was one of the first truly popular African American entertainers. He first came to prominence in the 1920s and remained popular until his death in 1971. A year after his performance, Armstrong hit the charts with "Mack the Knife." He won a Grammy in 1964 for "Hello Dolly." "He was an impressive man, a neat person," said Jim Spackman.

Billy May and His Orchestra came in 1952. May was a trumpet player during the big band era in the 1940s. He later became famous for composing film and television music for programs including the *Green Hornet*, *Batman* and *Naked City*.

Sauter-Finegan Orchestra played for one night in 1952. Eddie Sauter and Bill Finegan began recording and playing together in 1952 for RCA Victor. The two teamed up for a dozen hits in eight years.

Ray Anthony and His Orchestra came for one night. He was originally in the Glenn Miller Band and had a hit with a remake of one of Miller's songs in 1952. He went on to appear on television quite a bit in the early 1950s.

Woody Herman and the "Herman Herd" came to Indiana Beach in 1954. Herman had been one of the most famous bandleaders in the 1930s and 1940s. He often played music that was considered experimental at the time. He went on to be the featured performer at Super Bowl VII.

Harry James came in on Thursday, May 15. James led a swing band during the 1930s and 1940s. The trumpeter cut many singles and appeared in many movies before he ever got to Indiana Beach.

Stan Kenton returned with a different group that he called his Modern Men of Music. His large band had thirty-nine pieces, including sixteen strings, a woodwind section and two French horns. This was one of the largest music groups that ever assembled at Indiana Beach.

Other orchestras that performed in the '50s included Tony Prince and His Orchestra with Janice Becker; Tony Papa and His Orchestra; Wendy Swartz Orchestra; Jimmy Adami Orchestra; Ralph Flanagan Orchestra with Rita Haynes; Don Adams Orchestra; the Singing Winds; Johnny Kay and His Orchestra; Burton Schlie and His Orchestra; Joy Cayler and Her All-Girl Orchestra; Walter Loftiss Band; Larry Lonnie Band; Freddy Shafer's All-Girl Orchestra; the Jack Walsh Band (the old Al Cassidy Orchestra); Billy Lester Orchestra; Roy Gordon Orchestra; Lu George Orchestra; Hal Kern Orchestra; Mickey Isley Orchestra with Martha Nash; Buddy Morrow and his trombone featuring Betty Ann Steele; Ralph Marterie and His Orchestra; Buddy Pressner's Band from Merrillville upstate; Wayne Carr Orchestra with Ann Shear from the University of Illinois; Maxine and Her All-Male Orchestra; Ina Ray Hutton and Her All-Girl Orchestra, an unusual band consisting of seventeen beautiful girls; Cheerful Earfuls; Boyd Bennett and His Rockets; Johnny Rinaldo's Orchestra; Garry Gimes and the Four Spades; Bill Getzel and His Orchestra; and Bill Pappas Band from Chicago.

"They had dances out there every night," recalled Mel Dawson of Monticello a couple years ago. He and his wife, Betty, enjoyed the music and dancing.

After Indiana Beach closed on Labor Day 1954, Lake Shafer was drained of water in late September. Tom told the press that some sixty thousand spectators watched the water recede to the original channel of the Tippecanoe River from Indiana Beach. Scavenger fish were going to be removed from the lake. The lowering of the lake also made it possible for Tom to expand the park to the south by raising a submerged island. Thomas O'Connor had originally created the island, but when the lake was filled in, the island was covered by two feet of water. His miscalculation was called "O'Connor's Foley" by local people. Tom Spackman capitalized on O'Connor's misfortune. The new island was called Paradise Island, and a bridge would connect it to Indiana Beach. The bridge to Paradise Island was completed during the summer.

In 1956, the new feature at the park was the Terrainescope Observatory on Paradise Island. A terrainescope was much like a telescope but was used to see the surrounding area up close. It is no longer in use today.

One of the craziest promotions held at the park was a man being shot out of a cannon twice a day for a week in 1956. Joy Bailey recalled a promotion in the 1950s about aliens coming from space to Indiana Beach. "Dad put

The bridge to Paradise Island opened on April 28, 1955.

The Terrainescope Observatory in this postcard was built on Paradise Island for people to see a unique optical instrument. The ground floor was used as a gift shop and lobby.

up a sign that read, 'Welcome people from space,'" she said. "That was a promotional thing to get people to come to the park."

A new attraction at Indiana Beach in 1952 was a ten-mile sightseeing cruise for one dollar for adults and sixty-five cents for children. The beach prices were $0.60 for adults and $0.30 for children in the '50s. A season pass could be purchased for $1.50 for adults and $0.90 for children.

Tom continued bringing in talent to attract people to Indiana Beach. Pro wrestling came to the park on Mondays in 1953. The charge was one dollar to see the wrestlers, such as Dick the Bruiser. After his match, he ended up in the Roof Garden and drank too much. "It took my dad and three other

This was the entrance to the beach in the 1950s. The worker in the booth went by the nickname "Doc." *Courtesy Ruth Spackman Davis.*

guys to get him off the roof," remembered Linda Wilmot, whose father was Clarence Luse, a bartender at the park.

In 1957, Robert McClure was vacationing at Indiana Beach when he dove into shallow water and injured his neck. He was taken by ambulance to White County Memorial Hospital. Accidents were rare at Indiana Beach, but they did happen occasionally.

Indiana Beach announced that Richard Moberg from Chicago had been hired as the new chef in the Indiana Beach Hotel restaurant that featured country fried chicken, seafood, steaks and other choices.

In 1959, the Aqua Theater on the southern end of the park introduced a water ski show with eight performers. The skiers were trained by skiers from Cypress Gardens in Florida, according to Joy, who participated in the first show. A boat also jumped through fire in the night performance. At first, the ski show was put on by several Spackmans. Joy and Jim skied in the show at first and later Cathy. "When the ski show started, we had five girls," explained Joy. "We did all kinds of tricks. I did doubles." Indiana Beach ran the ski shows for more than ten years before deciding to hire a company to perform the task.

By 1954, Indiana Beach had forty-eight cottages for visitors in addition to hotel accommodations.

1960s

The shift to rock-and-roll music continued into the '60s, eroding orchestra offerings even more. Big-name bands from WGN in Chicago came in for one-night stands in the ballroom, which could hold up to three thousand fans. Also, different types of dance contests were offered. Entertainment moved to the Skyroom when it was completed during the era. More rides were constructed at Indiana Beach in the '60s to make it more interesting to visitors. More camping sites were added to the resort, along with more parking and another entrance. A paddlewheel boat provided better transportation to view Lake Shafer and the Norway Dam at the end of the era.

Some of the top rock singers in the country found their way to Indiana Beach in the '60s. Joe Luse of Monticello recalls the many rock-and-roll groups that came to the park in his younger days. "They'd stop here and play one night," said Luse, who has also worked about twenty years at Indiana Beach. "It was always packed."

The ski show was free to fans and featured girls in a line during one part of the show.

Indiana Beach became a live *American Bandstand* without Dick Clark. In fact, the Les Elgart Band, which produced "Bandstand Boogie," the theme song for *American Bandstand*, came to the ballroom for a one-night show in 1961. The band released a number of other albums for Columbia Records during this time.

The most famous group to perform in 1963 was the Beach Boys. The group, which had signed with Capitol Records in 1962, had already hit the big time with hits like "Surfin' Safari," "Surfer Girl" and "Little Deuce Coupe." It went on to become known as "America's Band" and was inducted into the Rock and Roll Hall of Fame in 1988 and has a star on the Hollywood Walk of Fame. A couple years later, the band appeared again at the park. Jim Spackman booked the group and remembers it well. "The Beach Boys played twice a night and in between sets they went and rode the go-carts," Jim said.

The go-cart track was built on Paradise Island in 1968. It is no longer there. *Courtesy Ruth Spackman Davis.*

In 1965, the Righteous Brothers played in the ballroom. Bobby Hatfield and Bill Medley had come to fame a couple years earlier with a blockbuster number-one hit the year before: "You've Lost That Lovin' Feelin'." The singers hit the charts with many of the songs and also cut some solo hits until Hatfield died in 2003.

Also in 1965, Gary Lewis and the Playboys came to play on August 6. They soared to the top of the charts that year with "This Diamond Ring." The group had many hits until it broke up in 1970.

Johnny Rivers also performed in 1965. The rock-and-roll singer started recording in 1957 and was well known before coming to Indiana Beach. He was best known for the song "Memphis" the year before coming. He's recorded many records and albums and continues to play.

A show in 1963 contained Lou Christie, Brian Hyland, Ronnie Cochran and the Kasuals. Christie topped the charts in March with the hit "Two Faces Have I" and had a number-one hit two years later with "Lightning Strikes." He went on to record fourteen more hits. Hyland's first hit was "Itsy Bitsy Teenie Weenie Yellow Polka Dot Bikini" in 1960. In all, he recorded twenty-four singles and nineteen albums.

The 1964 summer season started off with a blockbuster singer, Bobby Vee. The singer was an established recording star before coming out with a number-one hit in 1961, "Take Good Care of My Baby." He has had thirty-eight hits on the Hot 100 and recorded many albums.

The Kingsmen also came in 1965. They were best known for their hit "Louie, Louie," which reached number two on the charts for six straight weeks. They eventually had seven other hits on the Top 100. Admission was $2.75 (about $18.50 today).

Jan & Dean performed for one night in 1964. William Jan Berry and Dean Ormsby Torrence were very popular in the late 1950s through the 1960s. Their most successful tune was "Surf City," which topped the charts in 1963. They had sixteen Top 40 hits, including "The Little Old Lady from Pasadena" and "Dead Man's Curve."

The Rivieras, a dance combo for the teenage set, provided the music for the semifinals of the dance contest in 1962. The South Bend group was best known for its hit "California Sun," which made it to number five on the charts. It also recorded other hits like "Little Donna," "Rockin Robin" and "Let's Have a Party."

The Impalas performed a special show at Indiana Beach. The American doo-wop group was very popular in the late 1950s. The group was a one-hit wonder with "Sorry (I Ran All the Way Home)," which reached number two on the charts and sold more than one million records.

Linda Scott, a Canadian American singer, performed in the ballroom in 1962. She had a million-selling single, "I've Told Every Little Star," in 1961. She went on to record a dozen songs that hit the charts during her singing career, which lasted into the 1970s.

Jay and the Americans came with their own dancers to the ballroom in 1965 for two performances. The group was formed in 1960 and hit the charts two years later. It was best known for "Come a Little Bit Closer" and "Cara Mia" before it appeared at Indiana Beach. The group played together until 1973 and reunited in 2006.

The Byrds also came to perform in 1965. The group had formed the year before and hit the big time with two smash hits in 1965: "Mr. Tambourine Man" and "Turn! Turn! Turn!" The American rock band was extremely influential with its folk singing and psychedelic sound. It played into the mid-1970s and has had two reunions since then.

Sonny and Cher hit popularity in 1965, a year before they came to Indiana Beach, when they had five songs on the U.S. Billboard Top 20, including their number-one hit, "I Got You Babe." "I remember when Sonny and

Tom Spackman wanted something that shot water up in the air in the bathing area so that people on the Skyride would have a good seat to view it.

Cher were here," Ruth Spackman Davis said. "They were just a couple of kids. They came in their sheepskin vests and rode the Skyride. People didn't recognize them then. They were new."

Jim remembers them too. They rehearsed with the Dick Halleman Orchestra. "Cher didn't like them and told them so," Jim explained. "Sonny was very apologetic." The couple went on to greatness in music, television and movies before they split up. Sonny passed away in 1998, but Cher still performs. They have a star on the Hollywood Walk of Fame.

Another blockbuster duo to come that year was Simon & Garfunkel. They had a trio of hit records—"The Sound of Silence," "I Am a Rock" and "Homeward Bound"—before they arrived at Indiana Beach. They went on to win several Grammy awards and were inducted into the Rock and Roll Hall of Fame in 1990.

The Outsiders also came to play. The Cleveland, Ohio group is best known for its hit "Time Won't Let Me" earlier in 1966 before it appeared at Indiana Beach. It had three other hits that year and released a total of four albums. The group disbanded in 1968.

The Yardbirds made two appearances in the ballroom in 1966. The British rock band started in 1963 and rose to fame in the United States with its hit "For Your Love." The group had fifteen singles and twenty-one albums. It broke up in 1968 but re-formed in 1992 and is still playing.

The Lovin' Spoonful also appeared in the ballroom in 1966. The group formed in 1964 and rose to fame after its hit "Do You Believe in Magic" in 1965. The rock band had another dozen hits and recorded seven albums. It was inducted into the Rock and Roll Hall of Fame in 2000.

The Cyrkle came to Indiana Beach in 1966 after touring with the Beatles. It was best known for its hits "Turn Down Day" and "Red Rubber Ball." It played from 1961 to 1968 and had several hits.

Vic and the Versatiles' hit was "I Can't Wait 'Till Summer" with Barc Records.

The McCoys, who were famous for "Sloopy," also played at Indiana Beach that year.

Mitch Rider & the Detroit Wheels played two shows in 1966. The group was best known that year for recording "Devil With the Blue Dress On" and "Good Golly Miss Molly," which climbed to number four on the charts. Mitch went on to make two dozen albums in four decades.

Tony Bellus and his group came to the ballroom once. His hit song "The End of My Love" had reached eighth on the charts. He also had one other hit record, but his career went downhill after that.

Another famous group that came was the Buckinghams, who were a hit with the crowd. The Sunshine Pop band from Chicago was a top-selling act in 1966 as it hit number one in the charts with "Kind of a Drag." The group went on to record another six single hits and a dozen albums. It continues to play today.

Music Explosion also came to play the ballroom. The American garage rock band from Mansfield, Ohio, hit the charts that year with a number-two hit, "Little Bit O' Soul." However, this was one of those one-hit wonder groups.

Every Mother's Son played two shows in 1967. This was another one-hit wonder group with one album that rose to number six on the Billboard charts. It did appear in a two-part television episode of *The Man from U.N.C.L.E.*

Sam the Sham & the Pharaohs & the Shemettes also performed two shows. The group became famous in 1965 when its song "Wooly Bully" topped the charts at number two. The song ended up selling three million copies. The original Pharaohs were replaced, yet the new group went on to record more hits like "Lil' Red Riding Hood" in 1966. The whole group stayed together until the mid-1970s.

The famed Jefferson Airplane came in for one night on Fourth of July weekend in 1967. The San Francisco rock band formed in 1965 and rose to fame after its record *Surrealistic Pillow* was a success and sold millions. The group broke up in the early 1970s and re-formed as the Jefferson Starship in 1974.

The Strawberry Alarm Clock performed in 1968. The psychedelic rock band was made famous for its hit "Incense and Peppermint" the year before. The group went on to have five singles in the charts and is still playing today.

Wayne Cochran plus the CC Riders also played in 1968. The "White Knight of Soul," as he was sometimes referred to, wore outlandish outfits and cut several albums but never gained much success. The soul singer and his exhilarating group were a hit in Las Vegas. CC Riders acted as his backup group.

In July 1968, the Lemon Pipers came for two shows. The psychedelic pop band from Oxford, Ohio, was known for the number-one hit "Green Tambourine." The one-hit-wonder band was formed in 1966 and played until 1969.

The American Breed also performed in 1968. At the time, its hit "Bend Me, Shape Me" was on the U.S. Billboard Hot 100 chart. It rose to number five on the charts. The group from Cicero, Illinois, had five songs hit the charts in two years.

Then Big Brother & the Holding Company played for two shows in 1968. The group formed in 1965 and played psychedelic music. It had three songs in the Hot 100.

Indiana Beach closed out the 1969 season with a bang as the Iron Butterfly came to perform. More than two thousand people crowded into the ballroom to see the American psychedelic rock band that had the 1968 hit "In-A-Gadda-Da-Vida." The album sold more than thirty million copies. The group's dramatic sound was considered the beginning of the heavy metal era. After the concert, the teens rushed the stage to get autographs.

Record hops were held for the first time in 1960 and on Sunday evenings. Admission was fifty cents, and free treats were provided. When musical groups were not performing music, disc jockeys played records.

Big bands, rock groups and singers continued to be invited to Indiana Beach throughout the 1960s. The most famous singer in 1960 was Guy Lombardo. The Canadian American bandleader formed the Royal Canadians in the 1920s. After playing at Indiana Beach, he did America's CBS-TV special on New Year's Eve in the 1960s and 1970s. He earned the nickname "Mr. New Year's Eve."

The Four Lads came to play in 1960. The Canadian male quartet had many hits before it performed, including two number-two hits, "Moments to Remember" and "No, Not Much" in 1955.

The Limeliters performed twice in one night. The folk music trio had made appearances on the Ed Sullivan and Dinah Shore shows before coming to the resort. It released many singles through RCA Victor and is still active.

Famed trumpeter Al Hirt came to play in 1963 for $2.25 per person (about $17.00 today). He started hitting the charts with his albums in 1961. He actually became more famous starting the next year when his singles began topping the charts. Hirt passed away in 1999 with nineteen singles and forty albums to his credit.

Country music recording star Roger Miller played two shows in 1965. His hits "King of the Road" and "Dang Me" won many awards. He was a composer, singer and comedian who recorded more than one hundred singles and albums until he passed on in 1992. He was posthumously inducted into the Country Music Hall of Fame three years later.

Brenda Lee, another country western singer, came to sing in 1965. She was a childhood singer who rose to fame in 1958. She had many hits by the time she arrived at Indiana Beach, including "I Want to Be Wanted" and "Break It to Me Gently." She continues to perform.

The Chad Mitchell Trio made a special appearance. The folk singing group had eight singles on the charts but none in the Top 20. It also played satirical songs that criticized currents events like the Vietnam War. The trio broke up in 1967 and then reunited in 2005.

The Serendipity Singers played in the ballroom with the help of the Dick Halleman Orchestra. The American folk group had its debut single, "Don't Let the Rain Come Down (Crooked Little Man)," hit number six on the charts in May that year. It had four more singles in the charts and cut eleven albums.

The Velvet Infinity won the Battle of the Bands at Indiana Beach in 1968. A Kokomo rock group called the What won the Battle of the Bands in 1969 by beating out three other groups. The group would compete again at the end of the season, and the best band would get the first booking of the season in 1970.

The Roof Garden Lounge also provided entertainment in the '60s. Probably the most famous group that played there was Archie Bell & the Drells, which performed there in August. The American R&B quartet hit it big the next year with the hit record "Tighten Up." The African American group went on to record many hits until it broke up in 1980. Troy Shondel was another performer in the lounge who made it successful with one hit, "This Time." The Castaways were also a one-hit wonder group with "Liar, Liar." Other groups that played the Roof Garden Lounge were Galaxie

Five, Peggy Dawn, Crackerjack Quintet, Vice-Roys, Monarchs, Collegiates, Varitones, Sangri-Lads and Zenobia on the Hammond Organ.

Besides bands and orchestras, Indiana Beach started the Teen Talent Night and dance contests in 1962. The talent contest concluded with a $125.00 prize. Twist and limbo contests were held once a week, and cash prizes were also given at the end of the season. In 1963, the lineup in the ballroom was Ladies' Night on Monday night, Teen Dance on Tuesday night, mixed dancing on Wednesday night, Teen Talent Night on Thursday night, special appearances on Friday night, Over 21 Dance on Saturday night and Hootenanny and Dance Contest on Sunday night. Then at the end of the year, the contests ended with cash prizes. Admission to dances in the ballroom was free. Semiformal wear was required when regular bands played, and admission was $0.85 (about $4.00 today).

The groups that played for the teen dances included the WLS Hop with Bernie Allen, Kenny & Counts, the Impalas, Gary and the Escorts, Rockin' Cat-tels, Renegades, Chateaus, Sounds Unlimited, Idle Few, Whoops New Combo, Ronnie and the Rascals with 5 Cents, Outrage, Fabulous Other Five, Daze, Human Being and Boys Next Door. The Sangralads, a garage band made up of residents of Sangralea Valley Home in Walton, Indiana, also played teen dances, as did Chosen Few, a Detroit garage band. Friend & Lover was probably the best band of the batch, as the American folk-singing duo of Jim and Cathy Post had the hit single "Reach Out of the Darkness," which reached number ten on the U.S. Billboard Hot 100 in 1968. The couple also played in the Roof Garden Lounge like many of these groups.

At the teen dances, the teens were asked to dress neatly or not be admitted. They were warned, "No sweat shirts, black jackets, blue jeans, T-shirts, or short-shorts." The park also advertised the event by saying, "You must be under 21." Besides the good bands, a psychedelic light show was shown for the first time at Indiana Beach.

The year 1969 was the last big one for attracting big singers and bands to Indiana Beach. "Agents realized that ballrooms—the normal venue for musical entertainment, big bands and singing groups—had limited capacity and that stadiums had significantly more capacity, thus bigger financial payoffs," explained Tom Spackman Jr.

Many special events occurred at Indiana Beach in the '60s. The Indiana Beauty Contest was held in 1965 in the ballroom. The winner, Charlene Kratochvil from Kokomo, represented the state in the Miss U.S.A. Contest. One of the finalists was a local girl, Sharon Pancini of Monticello.

A boat parade began on Lake Shafer in 1963 and was held for several years. The first was held on Labor Day weekend in 1963. Tom presented trophies to the winners at Indiana Beach. Debbie Puterbaugh was named queen at the crowning ceremony at the beach as well.

The Jaycees sponsored the Lake Shafer Championship Boat Races in 1965 at Indiana Beach. Admission was a dollar for adults but free for children under age twelve.

Representative Charles A. Halleck (R-Ind.) was the grand marshal for the Mardi Gras Afloat Boat Parade and Festival at Indiana Beach held on Labor Day 1966 to mark the end of the season. He also crowned the "Queen of the Waterways."

The new features to the park in the '60s were a reconstructed Kiddyland, a gift shop, a summer-wear shop and a new dining place called the Patio. Also new was the *Shafer Queen*, a wooden-hulled paddlewheel boat built to resemble an old-fashioned river steamer. The big boat provided rides to park visitors several times a day and could carry up to one hundred passengers. The boat moved along at eight miles an hour. In 1969, the first wooden *Shafer Queen* was replaced by a larger, steel-hulled *Shafer Queen*. The boat was designed by Tom and built by master craftsman Bill Luse Sr., who happened to have a similar craft on Lake Freeman. The wooden *Shafer Queen* was parked along the pier and turned into a restaurant called the Pronto Princess. Some people got confused by this. When they boarded the new restaurant, they'd ask, "When is this boat going to leave?" It didn't.

The first *Shafer Queen* was built in 1961 of wood. An upgraded version replaced it and is still in use today.

In 1965, Indiana Beach opened a new campground containing 150 sites, including modern showers and restroom facilities for campers in tents and pickups. The Skyroom Restaurant also opened with floor-to-ceiling plate-glass windows to allow diners to see the park and the lake while they dined. And there was live music for the people who dined there in the evenings from 6:00 to 11:00 p.m. With the Roof Garden Lounge, Skyroom Restaurant and a Skyride, some people got confused. One person called and said, "You know that restaurant you have, the Skytop, Skyline, Roofview, Skyview, Rooftop Restaurant…"

To give Indiana Beach another entrance to the south (now the main entrance), the Spackmans built a four-hundred-foot suspension bridge in 1965 to connect it to the new south parking lot, which had once been a golf driving range. Indiana's longest suspension bridge opened at Indiana Beach in August. After the ribbon was cut, a carrier pigeon was released. It flew back to Indianapolis, and two hours and three minutes later, it arrived at the office of Lieutenant Governor Robert Rock with a message that the bridge was now open. The bridge was opened to foot traffic only. While the largest suspension bridge in the state is strong, it does bounce a little when people walk on it.

The suspension bridge was built in 1965 and is the longest one in Indiana. *Photo by author.*

The Antique Auto Ride is very popular with families. The cars are replicas of those from the early 1900s.

Roller skating came to an end in 1965, and bumper cars were added to the venue on the same floor. The attraction was called Dodg'em Cars. Another new attraction was the Antique Auto Ride. The cars were patterned after the Model A Ford of yesteryear. Jim Spackman now admits that he once drove a motorcycle on the track when he was a teenager.

A new ride in 1965 was the Skyride, which was like a ski lift that allowed two riders to go a quarter of a mile from one end of the park to the other and see all that Indiana Beach had to offer. The ride rose forty-five feet above the ground. It was designed by Tom and built by Bill Luse Sr. The Paratrooper ride also arrived at the park in 1967. The ride takes passengers high into the sky and then brings them back gently to earth. The family ride is still at the park today.

Concessionaires Lance and Bert Douglas built the Haunted House and opened it at Indiana Beach to scare visitors in 1968.

Demand necessitated the building of a new picnic pavilion in 1968 in order to provide more space. A go-cart track was built that year on Paradise Island. Luse also constructed the track.

The following year, another new attraction called the Mystery Mansion was constructed. The two-story ride through the dark had surprises to

Three children come out of the Dark Ride. The ride was remodeled and is now the Den of Lost Thieves. *Courtesy Ruth Spackman Davis.*

thrill riders. The name was changed later to Dark Ride and later still remodeled as the Den of Lost Thieves. Riders are now equipped with "guns" to take aim and bring the criminals to justice while scoring some "gold" along the way.

The advertising pitch was changed in the 1960s to "Indiana's Largest Privately Owned Summer Resort." In 1961, Indiana Beach advertised Chef Francis Conrad as the cook at the Beach House Dining Room. The restaurant featured seafood, prime rib, steak, pan-fried chicken and other specialties. Charlie Paulk was the manager of the restaurant. Carol Tewes, the owner of the Cottage Shops across the street from the park, remembers when culinary students from Joliet Junior College would do summer internships at the Skyroom Restaurant to get experience.

The park also advertised for jobs and got job applications from every state in the country and many foreign countries. At the time, the park employed more than five hundred people.

Something new in 1961 was an artists' and handicrafters' bazaar every Sunday afternoon in the ballroom. People were able to sell their wares all summer.

In the '60s, the Spackman family started thinking of making the shift to more rides for the whole family to enjoy, according to Ruth Davis. "When we had the rock bands, the crowds began to be very unfriendly," she explained. "We had to be a destination park."

Sometimes companies offered special days at Indiana Beach. For example, A&P grocery presented a Family Frolic Day at the park in August 1964. With a cash register receipt, people could save $0.75 on $1.25 worth of rides.

A heat wave came in early July 1963, and the park was packed on the Fourth of July. In fact, Tom told the press that a record crowd of thirty thousand visited the park on the holiday, including fifteen thousand for the fireworks show.

A couple tragedies occurred in the '60s. On July 3, 1960, a Sunday, an early morning thunderstorm led to the death of an Indiana Beach employee. Charles Edward McCully Jr., who was employed at the skating rink, was helping a boat concession operator round up boats when his boat was swamped by the storm under the bridge leading to Paradise Island. The empty boat was found with the lights still on by the Lakeview Home, just north of Indiana Beach. On the Fourth of July, police dragged the lake for his body, but their efforts were hampered by boaters and skiers. McCully's body was finally found about 6:00 a.m. the next day in the lake by two fishermen. McCully was a 1960 graduate of Buffalo High School.

The fireworks show began at Ideal Beach in 1930 on the Fourth of July. Nowadays, Indiana Beach does a fireworks show every Saturday like what is shown in this postcard.

In 1965, a youth who had been working as a bartender at Indiana Beach died in a car crash after work. It turned out that the Evansville youth, Nick Lemeke, was only twenty years old and shouldn't have been serving alcohol. The Alcoholic Beverage Commission decided to investigate the incident. The excise police also found two other bartenders who were only twenty years old at the park.

For the most part, the ski show went off without a problem at Indiana Beach. However, on July 14, 1969, that all changed. Water kite ski star Pat Dwyer was injured when his kite rope was cut when it caught on a wire. He dropped about twenty-five feet onto the cement and then fell into the swimming area. Dwyer sustained a three-and-a-half-inch cut on the back of his head and multiple bruises. He was taken to White County Memorial Hospital and listed in good condition soon after the accident. He recovered and continued to be a barefoot skier in the show for several years.

Law enforcement became an issue at the park in the '60s. The park employed off-duty police officers and others to work security at the park, but the local sheriff didn't think they were doing enough. In mid-July 1965, White County sheriff Leroy Farney decided to clamp down on juveniles breaking curfew at Indiana Beach and took twenty into custody. Tom Spackman disagreed with his action. He said that many of the young people were not

One of the thrilling acts in the ski show was the boat going through a wall of fire. *Courtesy Ruth Spackman Davis.*

from the local area. The sheriff released the youngsters to their parents if it was a first violation. Then later in July, Sheriff Farney arrested three youths from Indianapolis in the Roof Garden Lounge. They were carrying fake IDs. A White County justice of the peace fined them seventeen dollars each.

To make matters worse with problems at the park, a band that was playing in the Roof Garden Lounge had a member who was underage. To skirt the law, Larry Miller erected a platform across the tops of the two statues centering the two water fountains below the lounge and played there. The two statues were replicas of the tiki heads found on Easter Island. Jim Spackman constructed them using steel and concrete. The situation was resolved when the White County Court banned Miller from the state, so he was ordered to quit.

The sheriff continued making spot checks at the park to curb underage drinking and curfew violations for a month and arrested more than two hundred offenders. The continued harassment by the sheriff came to a boiling point on August 21. Sheriff Farney and Deputy Sheriff Jack Loy were at the resort taking five juveniles into custody for curfew violations when Farney got into an argument with Tom over Farney's police dog. Spackman accused the sheriff of harassment and claimed that it was not necessary for him to bother him, his employees or his customers. Tom wanted the sheriff to put his dog away, but the sheriff wouldn't do that. Dave Stimmel was there at the time and saw the confrontation. He said that Jim took photos of the arrest and Tom acted like he was being manhandled by the sheriff and his deputy. "It was hysterical," said Stimmel, who was seventeen at the time. "Tom was really putting it on for the camera."

Jim remembers the event as well and says, "I think he [the sheriff] was trying to get a payoff." The sheriff ended up arresting Tom that night and putting him in jail for resisting arrest and disorderly conduct. Tom was later released on a $100 bond.

On September 2, Alcoholic Beverage Commission judge Paul Lustgarden asked Sheriff Farney and Tom to work out their differences. "My recommendations will depend wholly upon the results of the sheriff's conference with you," Lustgarden said to Tom, according to the *Logansport Pharos-Tribune*. As a result of the meeting, Indiana Beach would get its own private police force of five who would be deputized by the sheriff and given police powers to make arrests. They could only arrest people who were in violation of the law at the park, and then they would turn over the accused to the sheriff to handle the case. The commission also put Indiana Beach on probation. After the 1966 season, the park was taken off probation.

Chapter 3

A TIME FOR CHANGE

1970s

Some amusement parks in the Midwest closed down in the late 1960s, such as Riverview Amusement Park in Chicago. However, Indiana Beach was reported by the media as still going strong by adding new rides each year and pulling in big crowds. To keep this trend going, Tom decided it was time for a change. He found out that people wanted bigger rides, like roller coasters.

The first roller coaster at Indiana Beach came in 1971 when the Galaxi was built of steel at the park. S.D.C. manufactured the coaster. It was built over the water. A Moon Bounce and Zugspitz were also added. This gave the park seventeen exciting rides. The first true family ride in the '70s was the Wabash Cannonball, a train that went from Kiddyland to the end of Paradise Island. The train started running in 1972.

In 1976, improvements for the season included new food service facilities, new shops and a large amusement game room.

Then in 1978, the Spider and Superstition Mountain were added to the park; however, Superstition Mountain didn't open until late June. The Flying Bobs came to the park in 1979 and is still there. A new water slide was put in the campgrounds.

Pay One Price (POP) for rides was introduced in 1971. On Saturday only, the cost for a POP was $2.50 (about $14.00 today). Admission to the park began for the first time in 1973. The park started charging $0.25 for admission in order to pay for the free ski show, according to Ruth. The ski

Tom Spackman examines the construction of Superstition Mountain in 1976.

show in 1971 featured the Delta Wing Nite Flyer and barefoot skiing through fire once in the afternoon and once in the evening. It went from two to three shows in 1973, so people had a choice of watching at 2:00 p.m., 5:00 p.m. or 8:30 p.m. Jenny Wilson of Daleville became a substitute in the ski show at age thirteen, one of the youngest skiers to ever perform in the show.

By the 1970s, Indiana Beach offered five hundred campsites, fifty motel and inn rooms and fifty modern cottages. When gas prices went down during the summer of 1979, camping increased some 28 to 35 percent at the campgrounds, according to manager Tim Hardy. "The length of stay here also increased with our becoming a one to two-week destination stop for many campers," he said, according to the *Logansport Pharos-Tribune*.

The big band era as well as the era of the top named rock-and-roll bands came to an end at the park in the 1970s. However, the park would still bring in Top 40 bands in the Roof Garden Lounge and small groups to entertain in the Skyroom. Occasionally, a named group or orchestra would play in the ballroom.

In 1971, teen dances began in late March at Indiana Beach. Groups that played on Saturday nights until the beach opened for the season included Firth Street, Buckwheat, Eden Rock, Joshua and Hitchcock Railroad.

During one part of the ski show, the men carried the women. Many of the shows had about ten acts. *Courtesy Ruth Spackman Davis.*

The big concert of 1971 came when SRC, Bob Seger, Teegarden & Van Winkle and Split Stones performed. SRC, short for Scot Richard Case, was a rock band from Detroit that recorded several records and albums; however, none were hits. Seger is an American rock singer-songwriter who has put together several groups and produced many records and albums, but he was on his own when he came to Indiana Beach. He's best known for the song "Night Moves," and he still performs today. Teegarden & Van Winkle was a duo composed of Skip Knape and David Teegarden. The folksy rock group is best known for "God, Love and Rock & Roll," which hit number twenty-two on the U.S. Billboard Hot 100 chart.

Alice Cooper also came in 1971. The American shock rock singer, songwriter and musician started performing in 1960, and he still continues to sing today. His breakthrough hit was "I'm Eighteen," which was released in 1971. He's recorded many singles and albums since. Cooper has also been in five movies.

Bloodrock performed in August 1971. The American hard rock band produced five albums that charted. None of its singles ever rose to fame.

Several orchestras still made appearances in the ballroom, such as Biddy Biddeson Orchestra, Bill Hall Orchestra, Joe Hoffman Orchestra, Invincibles Orchestra, Bob Norman Orchestra, Gib Gentry Band, Vala Lites and the Larry Mechem Orchestra. The Eddy Howard Orchestra was probably the best orchestra to play in the '70s. The American vocalist rose to fame in the 1940s with the hit "To Each His Own," which hit the top of the charts in 1946. The band played for five decades. The Tommy Wills Orchestra from Indianapolis was another good group. Wills, a saxophonist, cut a record called *Man with a Horn* in 1963 that sold half a million copies worldwide. In 1979, the ballroom was turned into the new Teen Disco Palace, which would be open on Friday and Saturday nights during the summer.

In the Roof Garden Lounge, many different groups played, including Lady & Friend, Happy Daze, Anything Goes, Wind, Easy Street, Cops & Robbers, Star Flight, Hot Ice, Peace & Love, Clean Sweep and Cicero Park, a British soul group. Probably the most famous small group that played in the lounge was the Charles Kenny Show. Kenny was the songwriter for "Love Letters in the Sand," which was made famous by Pat Boone in 1963. Also on the Roof Garden, a Boone's Farm Drinking Contest was held on Thursday nights, and a Beach Bunny of the Week contest was held every Friday night in 1972. An Amateur Go-Go Girl Contest was also held on Tuesdays.

In the Skyroom, the Bennetts started playing in 1972 and lasted there for many years to come. "A lot of people came to the Skyroom to see Jim and Linda Bennett," said Ruth Spackman Davis. The Skyroom offered

A free ferryboat began taking campers to and from the campground and Indiana Beach in 1970. *Courtesy Ruth Spackman Davis.*

a different special meal every night. Tuesday night was Party Night and Thursday night was Luau Night, featuring a limbo and hula contest. For Party Night on Tuesdays in the Skyroom, Indiana Beach suggested that you "bring your mother-in-law and do the bunny hop." Party Night included a twist contest.

To make it easier for campers to get to the park, a new ferryboat was offered in 1970 to carry campers for free from the campground to the Indiana Beach Boardwalk. Tom went to the Wisconsin Dells to find out how they were hauling people around. He wanted to bring in the duck rides at first, but they were expensive. Instead, he built another boat and then, later, a second one. When the boat went under the bridge on North West Shafer Drive, there wasn't a lot of clearance. "One day this little old lady got on the boat and crawled up to the driver and yelled, 'We're going to hit the bridge,'" explained Ruth.

The park also installed its own water system, and Tom put in outlets to get water from the lake and purchased fire hoses to fight any fires. He was at the park when the dance casino burned down in 1930 and didn't want something like that to happen again. The Monticello Fire Department was located about five miles away, and by the time officials arrived, a fire could be out of control.

By mid-July 1970, the male skiers for the ski show had dwindled and Indiana Beach had to advertise to get some more. They wanted experienced jumpers and offered room and board. They advertised again in August for cooks and salad girl jobs, paying $2.50 for cooks and $2.00 (about $12.00 today) for salad girls. Minimum wage at the time was $1.60 (about $9.75 today) in Indiana. Getting people to work at the end of the season was always a problem because high school teens went back to school in mid-August.

For the annual boat parade on Labor Day in 1970, U.S. congressman Richard Roudebush was one of the judges. He was running for reelection at the time.

The Indiana Gamma Chapter of the Delta Theta Chi Sorority held a convention at Indiana Beach in 1971. The park had great facilities to host conventions, especially during the off-season. The park could hold more than eight hundred overnight visitors.

Schools started sending busloads of students to Indiana Beach in May. This practice continues today.

A couple of special events were held in the 1970s at Indiana Beach. The Hollycast with WCFL disc jockey Dick Biondi presented a one-hour show on the history of rock-and-roll in the Roof Garden in early June. Biondi was an American Top 40 and Oldies disc jockey. He was known for his screaming delivery and wild antics.

In 1976, the *Shafer Queen* was decorated in red, white and blue in honor of the 200th birthday of the nation. Delco-Remy celebrated by holding a hot-air balloon race over Lake Shafer over Memorial Day weekend. It was promoted as the world's first over-the-water balloon retrieval race. It was also the last.

In April 1978, a Lake Shafer Run started at the Indiana Beach Campground. The run was eleven miles in length and circled the lake. The run was repeated for several years before it ran out of gas.

Indiana Beach sometimes remained open the weekend after Labor Day for a special weekend, a practice that continues today. An example was Indiana Beach Holiday, sponsored by Local 1312 USWA in 1972. The public was invited and could get in for just a dollar if they provided a coupon from the newspaper, which would allow them to go on rides all day from 10:00 a.m. to 6:00 p.m. A picnic was provided for union members.

Drug arrests started occurring at the park in the 1970s. In 1973, Indiana Beach security guard Bob Gnall apprehended six Chicago juveniles for possession of marijuana and alcohol and turned them over to the sheriff for disposition.

On March 1, 1975, President Tom Spackman announced the consolidation of three sister corporations into one. Mid West Amusement Corporation and Lakeside Operating Corporation would consolidate with Indiana Beach, Inc. The consolidation was made to simplify accounting and recordkeeping procedures. The new corporation would own all facets of Indiana Beach, containing 250 acres.

In the mid-1970s, one of Tom Spackman's teenage workers, Ed Ward, stopped him on the boardwalk and asked him if he could paint signs for the park. Tom's reply was, "You have to be as good as the sign painter now but do it for cheaper." So Ward started painting signs as good as the existing signs for a cheaper price. He did a few at first, and by 1985, he was painting all the billboards and many other signs in the park. He still paints signs for the park today. "He never discouraged young people; he encouraged them," said Ward about the owner. Ward met his wife, Sylvia Milligan, at Indiana Beach. She was running the bumper car ride. They've been married for more than forty years.

To help with education, Indiana Beach management announced a scholarship award program in May 1975 in which free tickets would go to students with high grades. Student getting As, Bs and Cs would be given rewards. The highest reward was eight dollars in tickets to a student with five As. A student had to bring his report card Monday through Friday to the park during June.

Special discount tickets were sometimes offered in the '70s. In 1977, Chesty Triple Pack Potato Chips had a special discount to the park.

A tragedy occurred in 1978 when a little girl drowned. The five-year-old child drowned while swimming at Indiana Beach on August 12. Rose Marie Salas reported her daughter, Monica Michelle, missing about 3:30 p.m. Her body was later found by lifeguards in three to four feet of water. She was declared dead at the scene at 7:09 p.m. She was from East Chicago and had been with her uncle.

"The kids were horsing around and hiding from the lifeguard," recalled Joe Seurynck, boardwalk supervisor. "He couldn't see them." There was a blind spot that the lifeguard couldn't see. "He told them once to get out of there."

1980s

Another roller coaster and other different rides were brought to Indiana Beach in the '80s. Also, the best marketing plan for the park was born during the era and remains today. Tom started advertising the park in the southern Chicago suburbs. "Half of our business comes from Illinois," Tom said in the *Logansport Pharos-Tribune*. Once again, Top 40 bands were brought in to entertain in the Roof Garden Lounge and ballroom. Admission was raised in 1982 to fifty cents and then a dollar in 1987. And a couple of fires brought small setbacks to the park in the era.

While the devastating fire in 1930 came at the beginning of the season, the fire that took the Haunted House came on the last day the park was open in 1980. The fire broke out soon after the park closed on Saturday night at midnight. Indiana Beach employees fought the blaze with their fire hoses, but there was no stopping it. "It was a wooden structure," explained Ruth.

The Monticello and Buffalo Fire Departments also responded to the fire, but it was a losing cause, and the structure was totally destroyed. The value of the building was set at $40,000. Assistant Fire Chief Robert Hickman recalled the fire, as that was his second year with the Monticello Fire

The Haunted House lasted for twelve years at Indiana Beach before it burned to the ground in 1980.

A couple enjoys the Tig'rr coaster, the second coaster built at Indiana Beach.

Department. "It was a hot fire," he remembered. "We contained it to the house only." The state fire marshal was called in to investigate the fire and could not determine a cause. The structure was built and owned by Lance and Bert Douglas, who moved to Florida after it burned down.

Fire struck the park again in 1982 and destroyed the campground grocery store and a pavilion. Contents were valued at $40,000 by Tom.

In 1980, a new Paratrooper ride began swinging over the water. The family ride spun around and glided riders with gentle turns.

The second roller coaster at Indiana Beach was built in 1984. The Tiger Coaster, later changed to Tig'rr, was designed by Jet Star and Anton Schwarzkopf of Germany and manufactured by his company, Schwarzkopf GmbH.

Dr. Frankenstein's Haunted Castle opened in 1983, replacing the burned-down Haunted House. Tom designed the castle and had it built of cement block so that it would look like a castle and wouldn't easily burn down.

The Rocky Rapids Log Flume ride opened in 1986 and became an immediate hit. The log flume goes through tunnels before taking a final plunge in cold rapid waters. The only hazard with the ride was that the passengers might get a little wet.

Joe Luse takes a ticket at the Rocky Rapids Log Flume ride. Luse has worked at the park for about twenty years. *Photo by author.*

In 1987, the new attraction was a water park that was put in to catch the latest trend in the park business. The water park featured an Action River and three water slides.

The Giant Gondola Wheel was constructed in 1989 and opened in July on Paradise Island. Each gondola carried six adults and gave them a panoramic view of Lake Shafer, Indiana Beach and the surrounding area. At night, the ride was covered with more than six thousand colored lights to light up the park.

Teen dances continued in the ballroom during the 1980s to DJ-spun music. In the Roof Garden, Top 40 bands like Empire, Marion Deaton Band, Spice, Florida, Angel's Flight and others performed. Deaton now does Willie Nelson tribute shows. Mostly couples played music in the Skyroom, like Bob and June Armstrong and Dan and Sandy McGraw, but some solo singers also performed, including Dan Wilhoite and Gary Branson. The Thirty-eighth Infantry Division Band of the U.S. Army National Guard presented a free concert in 1987.

The Giant Gondola Wheel ride rises high on Paradise Island, and the Hoosier Hurricane goes around it. *Photo by author.*

Indiana Beach offered several different promotions during the 1980s. The Lucky Las Vegas Days promotion in 1982 was the first, with prizes up to $1,000 in cash. People were given ten tries at a slot machine to win ride tickets or cash. The game was free. To celebrate the fifty-eighth anniversary of the park in 1983, hot dogs and Coke were a quarter each, as were the rides. The end-of-year fireworks show in 1983 featured a giant "Niagara Falls" suspended from a roller coaster seventy feet in the air. In 1984, if children brought their Cabbage Patch Kid, they would get two dollars off on a POP ride ticket. A Grissom Day was offered in 1987. Grissom Air Force Base is located less than an hour's drive from Indiana Beach. In 1989, Hook's Drug Stores offered discount tickets to Indiana Beach. This practice continues today, with Walgreens Drug Store offering discount tickets, as well as many other local businesses that sell the tickets for twenty-five dollars, a savings of eleven dollars for a combo ticket.

A new marketing campaign was launched in 1986 when the park celebrated its sixtieth anniversary. A mascot called I.B. Crow was created, along with the advertising slogan "There's more than corn in Indiana."

This entrance sign shows I.B. Crow. The character has been a hit at Indiana Beach. *Photo by author.*

The uncanny success of the campaign brought new visitors to Indiana Beach from all over the Midwest, and attendance rose to half a million visitors a year.

The '80s were not without some drama. A ten-year-old boy was stranded on the Skyride at Indiana Beach in 1981 when a quick-moving thunderstorm hit and cut the power. The Monticello Fire Department responded and retrieved the boy using an aerial truck. The boy was wet, cold and frightened but unharmed by the storm. The park usually gets patrons out of harm's way before thunderstorms threaten the park.

In 1988, an Illinois man was injured in the Indiana Beach Campground when an M80 firecracker exploded in his hand. Steve T. Pollack of Hazel Crest, Illinois, received a massive injury to his left hand and was taken to St. Elizabeth's Hospital in Lafayette.

During the '80s, some crime did occur at Indiana Beach. The park employed security officers who wandered the park looking for any trouble. Occasionally there was trouble at teen dances or in the bar after someone had too much to drink, but the beach was generally a very safe place to be.

However, the first crime occurred in 1981 when four men were arrested for breaking into a pinball machine in the Game Barn. They were from Indianapolis, and one was a juvenile.

The following year, an Indiana Beach security guard was hit in the head by someone who was trying to steal gasoline at 3:00 a.m. When the guard asked the man what he was doing, he said he was getting gas for the ferryboat; however, the boat runs on diesel. That's when the guard was struck from behind by another man. Then the men fled in a motorboat.

On August 12, 1984, a fight in the parking lot of Indiana Beach resulted in a Lafayette man being shot in the head and a Kokomo man being severely beaten in the head. Charles E. Roundtree of Lafayette later died from the head wound. James Cannon, from Kokomo, suffered facial injuries and was sent to the hospital for treatment. Cannon was later charged with battery with a deadly weapon, while Roy Roundtree and Robert Brummett were charged with battery causing serious bodily injury. Cannon ended up with a jail sentence of twenty weekends at the White County Jail and a fine of $131 plus $50 a month. Brummett pleaded guilty to a Class A misdemeanor and was credited for his eighteen days in jail. He didn't have to serve any other time. Roundtree's case was dismissed.

On Christmas Eve 1987, three adults and two juveniles were arrested for burglary at Indiana Beach Campground Store, which was closed for the season.

As far as special events, the Lake Shafer Jet Ski Races were held at Indiana Beach in 1986. This was part of a ten-race series by the International Jet Ski Boating Association that lasted a few years at the park.

By the late 1980s, the park employed more than seven hundred employees during the summer. Ruth Spackman Davis hired teens starting at age fourteen. To fill the void left when the teens went back to high school in mid-August, she started hiring young people from other countries. Today, the practice continues, and many youngsters from Jamaica came to work at the park in 2013.

1990s

The largest roller coaster in the park and some other rides began at the park during the 1990s. The campground was expanded to accommodate the increase in campers and recreational vehicles coming to Indiana Beach.

The Twister Thrill Ride was removed from the park in 1997. A sign warned customers, "This ride may cause dizziness, cars spin." *Courtesy Ruth Spackman Davis.*

A night boat parade began at the end of the era. The park opened on the weekends beginning in May and opened for the season on Memorial Day weekend. Then it closed to the public on Labor Day. Wabash National would rent the park the weekend after Labor Day for its employees. General admission at the park rose to $1.50 in 1995.

The new attractions in 1990 were the Falling Star ride, Boat Tag and Convoy Race. The Falling Star and Boat Tag were located on the south side of the boardwalk, which Indiana Beach had extended. The Falling Star ride is like a platform that goes up seventy feet in a circle at a faster and faster rate and then reverses the cycle. The centrifugal force throws passengers side to side. In the Boat Tag ride, patrons could ride in the two-person boats and compete against each other by maneuvering their boat and firing racquetballs. Hits on designated targets incapacitated guns or motion, adding to the challenge. Adding to the excitement area was a gallery of guns, which spectators use to fire at the boats and targets. These triggered spectacular geysers illuminated by colored lights. Meanwhile, an

People enjoy going down the Lazy River after coming down one of the slides in the water park. *Courtesy Ruth Spackman Davis.*

armored train car with four gunners aboard shuttled back and forth in the background to offer more targets for the boats and spectators. Convoy Race was a seven-car ride designed for smaller children and traveled in convoy for more than 960 square feet.

In 1992, the water park was expanded with the addition of two new tube slides and three hundred more feet to the Action River to make it a quarter mile in length. Water Swings was added to Indiana Beach during that year too. The ride was located on Paradise Island next to where the ski show is performed.

When the Hoosier Hurricane was built in 1994, it became the first wooden roller coaster built in Indiana in fifty years. The three-thousand-foot coaster reached a peak of one hundred feet, allowing for a very fast ride: fifty-five miles per hour on the highest descent. The coaster was designed and manufactured as an out-and-back coaster by Custom Coasters, Inc. (CCI). It was quite a challenge to build at Indiana Beach because of the space limitations of the park. This was CCI's first project using a steel superstructure, and there were some difficulties. Some things didn't fit quite well, and some extra welding had to be done. Also, the pilings were done by Bill Luse Sr. He did them in the wintertime, with temperatures dipping as low as twenty below zero.

Luse had to break through the ice several times to drive the pilings. Construction was held up sometimes because of the cold. Some of the pilings had to go down as deep as ninety feet. Despite the difficulties and the problems, the coaster opened only a week late. The cost of the coaster was $4.5 million. This made it the single largest investment in park history. Tom turned eighty when the coaster was put in, and he thought it would increase visitors to the park by 10 to 25 percent. At the time, the park was pulling in an estimated attendance of 650,000 to 700,000 annually.

The Sky Coaster Thrill Ride was added in 1995. The ride was constructed to give the riders the thrill of sky diving and hang gliding as they drop 110 feet. Tom actually tried the ride at a different park before he bought one for Indiana Beach. Usually when a ride came into service, Tom was the first one on it, like a test pilot in a new plane.

The Hoosier Hurricane roller coaster is one of the most popular rides at Indiana Beach. *Courtesy Ruth Spackman Davis.*

Parasailing was offered at Indiana Beach in 1996. Gene Sola of Goodland ran Fly High Parasailing there. The cost was forty dollars for a twelve-minute ride. People would go up as high as three hundred feet and be able to see for miles.

The new ride for 1998 was the Big Flush Water Coaster in the water park. The coaster offered two tunnels: the wicked twists of the blue tunnel or the surprises of the black tunnel.

In 1995, almost an acre of lake was filled in to give Indiana Beach more room for additional rides and attractions in the coming years. Since all the property around the park was owned by someone else, it was the only way the park could expand. This expansion resulted in the Frog Hopper and Double Shot rides being installed at the far north end of the park next to the water park in 1998. The two rides were located next to

The Double Shot is an intense up-and-down ride and takes people up eighty feet. *Photo by author.*

each other and provided vertical thrills to everyone in the family, as the grown-ups could take the Double Shot and the smaller children could ride the Frog Hopper.

The ski show ran four times a day in the 1990s. The water park was open from 10:00 a.m. to 6:00 p.m. daily, with the rides running from 11:00 a.m. to 11:00 p.m.

A local newspaper and Indiana Beach sponsored an electric boat parade on Lake Shafer. Electric meant the boats would be lighted and the parade would be run at night to provide a light show on the water. A Spring Festival and Craft Show were run in conjunction with the parade at the park in 1998.

The Roof Garden Lounge only featured local or state bands in the 1990s. One of the groups was Davis Farm, consisting of local musicians Bill McFadden, Scott Haygood and Mike Staggs.

As far as special events, the Monticello Jaycees and Purdue Fishing Club sponsored the annual March of Dimes Bass Team Tournament in September 1993. The competition was launched from the Indiana Beach Campground ramp. Another special event was the Back Home in Indiana spring festival held at Indiana Beach beginning in 1998. A craft show on the boardwalk featured about fifty booths. The Indianapolis Colts' "Care-A-Van" made a stop both days of the festival. A half dozen players signed autographs. A lighted boat parade was provided in the evening. The parade raised money for a proposed White-Carroll Family YMCA.

To help accommodate the growing RV market, two hundred primitive camping sites were converted to RV sites complete with electricity and running water in 1995. "We're trying to meet the demand for the RV market and also the demand for the pop-up campers," said manager Tim Hardy. He had been the manager for twenty-four years prior to this. About half the camping sites were now wired for cable television. A total of 88 employees were needed during the summer just to run the campgrounds. Then the Yogi Bear Jellystone Camp Resort opened in 1998. The resort contained 126 campsites, a swimming pool and three restroom facilities complete with washers and dryers. The addition of the new camp provided Indiana Beach 1,600 campsites to offer. Plus, the cottages and hotel could accommodate another 800 people. By then, the park was attracting nearly 800,000 visitors a year. About half of them came from out of state. The Yogi Bear and Indiana Beach Campground guests were provided free bus or ferry service to the Indiana Beach Boardwalk and free gate admission. Three more camper cabins were added to the camp resort in 1999 as well. With that addition, the resort now had 3 six-person cabins, 5 four-person cabins and 3 eight-person cabins. Each was equipped with plenty of storage space, a picnic table on the porch, a charcoal grill in the yard and electricity for radios and televisions. People had to provide their own bed linens and bath towels, but they could rent them as well.

During the summer of 1998, E. coli levels were especially high in Lake Shafer, but this had no effect on Indiana Beach, as its swimming area is spring fed. Plus, the resort wasn't contributing to any problems in the lake because it had its own sewage system installed two decades before. Word spread about the problem in Lake Shafer, which led someone to call Indiana Beach and say, "I heard you're closed because of E. coli." Actually, it was some tributaries to Lake Shafer that had high readings. "The quality of the lake is very good but it takes a while to get that message across," Tom Spackman Jr., general manager, told the *Logansport Pharos-Tribune*.

2000s

The new century marked the seventy-fifth anniversary of Indiana Beach, and the Spackman family went all out to make the occasion a special birthday celebration. The saying used that year was "Life's a Beach… Two Men, a Dream and a Crow." Two more roller coasters and new rides brought more thrills to Indiana Beach in the new century. In 2001, the Spackmans decided to look for a buyer for their amusement park, according to Cathy (Spackman) Juntgen in a *Lafayette Journal Courier* article. The end of the decade meant the end of an era, as the Spackman family sold Indiana Beach in 2008.

During the special birthday of the park in 2000, the television show *Across Indiana* came out to film a segment. Gary Harrison told viewers that Indiana Beach was north of Indianapolis and south of Lake Michigan. "If you can't have fun here, you can't have fun," he said.

At one point in the filming, Harrison and general manager Tom Spackman Jr., the owner's son, stopped in front of the Tilt-A-Whirl. "More people lose their lunch on this ride than any other ride in the park," explained Tom. "We keep a hose here just for that purpose."

Harrison asked Tom Jr. what he would like to see in people, and he responded, "I think it's the satisfaction of seeing families going home with smiles on their faces and really enjoying the day spent with us."

This postcard shows the suspension bridge, Paradise Island and all of Indiana Beach as it looked in 2000.

The annual electric boat parade was called the "Diamond Jubilee: 75 Years of Indiana Beach Memories."

The park also ran a contest for local schoolchildren to make posters about Indiana Beach for the celebration. Winners were put in a newspaper supplement. Cash prizes of $500, $300 and $50 were provided.

In 2001, Indiana Beach constructed another roller coaster called the Cornball Express. The 100-foot-tall coaster cost $2.6 million to build. The new 2,100-foot-long coaster had a steel frame and wooden track. To celebrate the ride, Indiana Beach created another mascot called Cornball Jones. Some neighbors complained about the coaster after it started running, but to no avail, as the government allowed the beach to continue the ride. With the park bringing in about $50 million to the local economy, shutting down the park would be devastating to the county. Another attraction that was added in 2001 was a rock-climbing wall.

The Superstition Mountain ride was removed in 2002, but the building structure remained and was replaced with the Lost Coaster of Superstition Mountain. Tom Sr. designed the coaster, CCI manufactured the ride and Bill Luse Sr. constructed it. The coaster had an elevator lift to take people to the highest point. Then it would weave its way down into a cave and through a mountain to the end. During the fast, dark ride, passengers encounter wild

The rock-climbing wall was put along the boardwalk at first and is now located in Adventure Point. *Photo by author.*

animals, falling rocks and other thrills. Built on Paradise Island next to the Taco Shoppe, the new ride immediately became popular. The Lost Coaster was voted the best coaster built in the world that year.

In 2004, the new ride at Indiana Beach was the Air Crow, located over the water. "It is a rider-controlled ride, where you can control the height," general manager Tom Jr. told the press.

A Mini Pirate Ship was constructed in 2005 to provide another ride for youngsters and their parents.

Splash Bash came to Indiana Beach in 2006. The name was later changed to Splash Battle. The attraction replaced the Boat Tag on Paradise Island. The ride allows people to ride a "battleship" and shoot water at opponents.

The new attraction in 2007 was a motion picture theater that would show 3-D movies and have moving seats. One of its movies was about dinosaurs. It was located between the Double Shot and the Big Flush.

Dr. Frankenstein's Haunted Castle was recognized as the best walkthrough and funhouse attraction by Darkride and Funhouse enthusiasts in its fifth annual members' survey. The funhouse was first built in 1983 after the previous funhouse burned down. The castle was renovated in 2000.

One of the special events that has turned into an annual affair is Academic Days, which began in 2000. Students from twenty-five schools come to Indiana Beach in late May for three days to ride coasters in the inaugural Physics Day at the park to experience physics in action. Cooking was added to the annual Academic Days program in 2005, which was in its fifth year at the park. It was held as a precursor to the summer opening, and students got to learn about cooking at the restaurants at Indiana Beach.

Indiana Beach was also involved in Junior Achievement and various activities in Twin Lakes schools, like the program called "What Would You Do to Go to Indiana Beach?" Students could earn passes to the park if they met achievement goals. In 2003, the park started a new recycling program called "Whatever Floats Your Boat." Area children built boats out of empty soft drink containers. After building their crafts from recycled material, the children raced their boats on the Action River.

Indiana Beach also began Multiples Family and Friends Day in 2004.

In 2003, the seventh annual lighted boat parade was called "A Water Wonderland" and was held the weekend before Indiana Beach was set to open for the summer season. The parade offered $2,500 in prizes. This was the last year for the boat parade.

By the end of 2006, park attendance was reaching more than 800,000.

The Dance Club, open to young adults ages thirteen to twenty, and Teen Disco were provided on Friday and Saturday nights in the ballroom until that ended later in the decade.

During the decade, Indiana Beach became the top employer in White County with about 1,200 employees. For many teens in the area, it became a rite of passage to work there during the summer months to earn some money and get some work experience locally. For many, it was their first job. The park also relied on summertime employees from countries from all over the world, including England, Ireland, France, China, Russia and Belarus. The park would give workers a place to stay as well as a job to do. Volunteer groups also pitched in to help out, like the Monticello Kiwanis, Rotary Club of Monticello and others. They did this to raise money for their clubs and help out the park with many tasks, such as picnics.

In the off-season in 2005, air conditioners were added to ten cabins at the Yogi Bear Jellystone Camp Resort.

In 2005, Indiana Beach celebrated its eightieth anniversary. The Spackmans took the occasion to promote the park with some specials. On a couple days, they rolled back the prices to provide rides for just a quarter after 4:00 p.m. On a couple other days, they rolled the price back to eighty cents for a POP during the evening session.

Cabins have been added to Yogi Bear Jellystone Camp Resort gradually. *Courtesy Ruth Spackman Davis.*

"Without Indiana Beach, we would be like any other rural community," said Mayor Bob Fox in the *Monticello Herald Journal*. "It's provided a tremendous service to this area."

"Things have changed quite a bit since the time when I watched Sonny and Cher perform here, but our goal of being a great family destination remains the same," said Ruth, the operations manager at the time, in the *Monticello Herald Journal*.

To handle the demand for more luxury living quarters, four new duplexes were constructed in the off-season in 2006. "They were extremely popular last year," said Tom Spackman Jr.

A couple new cottage units were added to Indiana Beach, and some were made handicap accessible. Two new cabins were added to Yogi Bear Jellystone Camp Resort as well. A fun park was added to the campground, and a Honey Creek Mining Operation was put between the two RV parks.

The ski show took on a pirate theme in 2007. Called "Pirates Revolt," it ran until 2013.

The Chaos ride was removed from the park in 2007. The main gate of the park was also remodeled that year.

Chapter 4

THE SPACKMAN FAMILY SELLS THE PARK

The decision to sell the park came in 2001, but it took another seven years before that happened. The decision came because Tom was getting up in age. His memory wasn't like it used to be. Plus, the park had become so large that it was no longer feasible for a family to run it. Several of Tom's five children were also getting up into retirement age as well.

After eighty-two years of ownership, the Spackman family sold their family amusement park in February 2008 to Morgan RV, ending years of rumors that they were going to sell it. The sale had been in the works since December 2007. The amount of the sale price was undisclosed. The announcement of the sale came in February in the local newspapers. "It's a little bit of a different turn for Morgan RV, but it's the way the company has been growing for the past six or seven years," said Morgan spokesman Debbie Evans, according to the *Monticello Herald Journal*.

At the time of the sale, the park had twenty-eight adult rides, nine children's rides, a fun house, shops, miniature golf, a water park, two pools, restaurants, two campgrounds and resort accommodations.

The first thing the new owners did to change the park was to give it a new paint job. That started in February using a number of local contractors and some park employees. Flamboyant colors were used to brighten up the park. Pinks, light blues and other colors were used on the water ride, ski ride and other rides throughout the park to make it look more presentable.

A new coaster, the Steel Hawg, was added to the park. It was manufactured by S&S. The ride wasn't ready until July, but it was a welcome addition to the

Benjamin Flatter of Lawrence, Indiana, enjoys spinning around on the Music Express. *Photo by author.*

park. Riders are taken up ten stories. The first drop is 111 degrees, making it the steepest ride in the United States when it was first built.

Two new buildings were constructed on the boardwalk to house games of fun, like you find at some carnivals. Unfortunately, they blocked one side of a natural attraction at the park, the "buglefish" or carp that people would feed with fish food, popcorn or other treats. Hundreds of the fish gathered, and people enjoyed watching the feeding frenzy that occurred. A few years later, the park reopened one side of the attraction and sold fish food instead of using the coin-operated machines of the past.

The other change was to close the inside sales booths and sell ride tickets at the entrance instead. However, this created long lines at both entrances to the park.

The new owners kept some Spackman family members around to act as advisors on staff to make the transition smoother. However, they did hire new employees who had no experience at the park, and this caused some jealousy and anxiety among the local employees who had been with

People from around the world such as this Japanese student, Ami Hisai, love feeding the carp, called buglefish. With her is the author's wife, Janice Madden. *Photo by author.*

the park for years and now found themselves working for a stranger from out of town.

The other change that was not liked by some local people was the loss of their full-time jobs. The park fired many employees and hired some back as part-time employees at the same or lesser rates. As a result, they lost some employees who needed full-time jobs. "A lot of people didn't come back," said Bill VanDeman. He also lost his salaried position, but he came back for a couple seasons before retiring.

The high-priced chefs were let go in favor of part-time cooks, which affected the meal choices at the daily buffet at the Skyroom Restaurant. However, the

The Cool Cash Card was implemented in 2009. It is like a debit card, and people add cash to it.

park did lower the prices a little. Still, some local clubs, like the Monticello Kiwanis, stopped going to the restaurant as a matter of protest.

With the downturn in the economy, General Manager John Collins decided to offer free general admission all season long in 2009. The last time it had been free to get into Indiana Beach was in 1972. "We hope the economy is on its way back up, but at the same time we understand the effect on families, and we hope to make it more affordable to come to the park," he said, according to a *Monticello Herald Journal* article.

Another change was implementing a cashless system called the Cool Cash Card. Visitors would purchase the card for twenty-five dollars and then use it to spend on games, rides and arcades. The park still offered a POP ticket for rides and combination water park.

The park opened the first weekend of May with a Cinco de Mayo celebration to attract the Hispanic population. The Taco Shoppe was also offering a taco-eating contest.

2010s

Morgan RV management decided to do something different and introduced season passes for the first time. The ski show changed its theme. Millions of dollars were spent on renovations to the hotel and other areas of the park.

For the first time since 1933, Indiana Beach offered season passes for patrons in 2010. The cost for a season pass was $99.95 for an individual; however, if someone purchased four at one time, the price dropped to $59.95.

Patrons were issued identification cards with their photos. The season pass price was lowered to $69.95 in 2013. At the beginning of 2014, the season pass price was $45.95 for six days. Season pass holders also get special deals on special days throughout the season, such as a ride on the zip line for only $5.00. Season passes were not transferable.

Free admission to the park was continued in 2010. Some parents took advantage of the offer by dumping off their children at the park for the day, so the park became like a babysitter. Then in 2011, the price for just entering the park was set at $3.50. People who lived in White County could get in free—a $3.50 savings—if they showed a library card or driver's license.

The Indiana Beach RV Park was renamed the NASCAR RV Resort in 2010 by Morgan RV. Only one in thirteen RV parks in the country had the brand name. Live broadcasts of NASCAR races were shown on large-screen projections at Rally Field. The Yogi Bear Jellystone Camp Resort was renamed Ideal Park in 2012. Yogi Bear would no longer be one of the mascots for Indiana Beach.

Indiana Beach did a lot of renovating in 2011. Some rides were moved around to make room for the new Adventure Point. The Flying Bobs, Water

Visitors to Adventure Point like climbing on the Sky Trail Voyager. *Photo by author.*

A person comes to the end of the zip line on Paradise Island after being launched from the front entrance of Indiana Beach. *Photo by author.*

Swings and the Falling Star were moved to the west side of the park. The new attraction included a zip line, a high rope challenge called the Sky Trail Voyager, a rock-climbing wall and the Adventure Point Outfitters Shop.

A new zip line was installed between the island and the main land parallel to the suspension bridge; however, it wasn't ready until August. Zip lines were coming into vogue all around the United States. The addition of the zip line marked the end of the miniature golf course on the island.

During the 2011 season, the *Shafer Queen* nearly had an accident with a pontoon boat, but pilot Steve Snyder avoided it through some quick actions. As he was docking the big paddleboat, a crewman spotted the pontoon boat coming on a collision course. Snyder put the paddleboat into reverse and hit the horn. The pontoon boat captain turned hard and glanced off the *Shafer Queen* to avoid the disaster. It would have been sort of like a car versus a semi-truck. In any case, the pontoon boat pilot didn't bother to stop and left the scene. Snyder reported the incident to the Department of Natural Resources, but it failed to catch up with the pontoon boat pilot.

Steve Snyder steers the *Shafer Queen* during a cruise on Lake Shafer. Snyder also gives the riders historical information about the park. *Photo by author.*

After an employee was fired in August 2011, some disgruntled employees protested outside the park about the firing and the safety of the rides. One of the signs said, "Bring Spacks Back." This prompted a visit by an inspector of the Indiana Department of Homeland Security to see if the rides were safe. An onsite check of the rides validated that they were indeed safe.

Some employees protested again on Labor Day weekend for two days. This time it was over employment practices and parking fees. These were the first instances of protest at the park.

On March 13, 2012, two roller coaster groups visited the park to see the coasters in the off-season, as Indiana Beach offers tours to groups. The groups came from ThrillNetwork.com and Sex, Drugs and Roller Coasters. They were given the tour by Sherry Vogel, the marketing and public relations manager. They were also given demonstrations of the Hoosier Hurricane and Cornball Express and a tour of the inside of the machine room to the Steel Hawg. The visitors also saw how the cars for the Steel Hawg are given rehabilitation in the off-season. Vogel said it cost the park about $99,000 to rehabilitate the cars.

As usual, Indiana Beach opened for weekends starting on May 11, 2012. Everything was open except the beach, which wouldn't open until Memorial Day weekend. The ski show would start on June 15. A season pass was $69.95, and it would include the rock wall and ropes course. People had to pay extra for the zip line.

In 2012, Indiana Beach closed the last remaining miniature golf course. The course was behind the beach area, so the owners replaced it with cabanas that could be rented for seventy-five dollars a day.

Morgan RV started trying to sell timeshares at its resorts in 2012. Workers with shirts saying "Ideal Private Resorts" walked around the park and asked people if they would be interested in hearing about the offer for a fifty-dollar Indiana Beach card. The timeshares were available at a dozen RV parks owned by the corporation in the Midwest and East.

The timeshares were like trailers, as they were mobile and could be moved from place to place. Several had been moved into Indiana Beach and could be rented on a daily basis for $313.39 for one person. There was a charge of $6.00 for each additional person, and it held up to six people.

These trailers first came to Indiana Beach in 2012. They are liked by families and provide more privacy than the hotel. *Photo by author.*

In 2013, renovations were made to the Indiana Beach Hotel. The interiors were gutted, and everything new was added. By this time, all the new trailers brought in the year before were ready for occupancy.

The Roof Garden Lounge was also renovated to modernize it. Flat-screen television and other improvements were made. During the season, "Indiana Beach Idol" was held on Tuesday nights, with prizes going to the winners. People would sing songs for the judges. Some groups that appeared in the lounge in 2013 were Ezra, Dear Abby, Bad Advice and Duke Tomato.

A change in 2013 was making the south entrance the main entrance to the park. Four ticket booths with windows on either side were set up to help sell tickets to people entering the park. This was an effort to make the process smoother and eliminate the long lines of the past with the new system of selling all the tickets for rides and water park when someone enters the park.

The park offered a number of promotions and sold tickets online, so sometimes this caused confusion at the ticket counter and led to disagreements. Ticket salesman Ted Van Rijk said there was one lady who had some free tickets but didn't use them because she wanted more, although it was a buy-one-get-one-free offer. He asked her why she didn't use a free ticket, and she replied, "I paid for admission so I could get another yellow ticket [free pass]." Then there was a person who bought a ticket online but still wanted to get one free ticket. "You can't get a discount on a discount," Ted explained to that person.

Banners were put up along the boardwalk that the ski show was the "World's Longest Running Ski Show." The show had started back in 1959, so it had been going on for fifty-five years. However, the show had changed quite a bit from the early days. A new company was hired to conduct what it called the Water Stunt Show in 2013. The ski stage was renovated. Lithgow Motor Sports also was a sponsor for the show and raffled off a SeaDoo. Profits raised were donated to the Give Kids the Gift Foundation.

Marketing manager Sherry Vogel gave away hundreds of free daily ride and water park tickets on several Fridays at the local radio station, WMRS. She also gave away tickets to the local media to get some local advertising, as the corporation didn't give her any money to advertise locally. It put its money in television and other Midwest advertising.

At any given time, some rides were down, which disappointed some patrons who were looking forward to riding them. Unfortunately, the Splash Battle attraction was down the whole year in 2013.

In 2012, a Haunted Trail was offered at the Indiana Beach Campground. All proceeds went to the White County Food Pantry.

The Splash Battle attraction was down all year in 2013. *Photo by author.*

In October 2013, eight employees were let go, and the office at Indiana Beach was closed. Vogel was one of those laid off, and she was certainly disappointed. Maintenance workers continued to work during the winter, and four of them attended the National Association of Amusement Ride Safety Officials in January 2014.

At the end of 2013, rumors surfaced that the park was going to close, so the *Lafayette Journal Courier* did a story about that possibility. General Manager Bob Gallagher dispelled that rumor by telling the newspaper, "We're planning for the 2014 season and actually looking forward to announcing some expansions."

In the same newspaper story, owner Bob Moser said all the closing rumors were false. "We're trying, we really are…You're not going to make everyone happy, but I'm trying here."

The closing of the park would be devastating to the local economy, since the economic impact of the park has been estimated at $60.4 million a year, according to Janet Dold of the Greater Monticello Chamber of Commerce. "It would be horrible," said Randy Mitchell, president of White County Economic Development.

Three new rides will be coming to Indiana Beach in 2014, according to an unnamed employee.

In January 2014, Indiana Beach's Facebook page had more than 51,000 likes.

In 2014, Indiana Beach will open for weekends on May 10. Then it will open for the season on May 23 and run until September 1, Labor Day. The water park will open daily beginning on May 24.

The most popular rides are the roller coasters at Indiana Beach, according to Joe Seurynck, boardwalk manager. Below is a list of rides and attractions at Indiana Beach and their first year at the park.

LIST OF RIDES AND ATTRACTIONS

Year	Ride/Attraction
1926	Beach, rowboats
1927	Toboggan
1930	Ferris wheel, merry-go-round (concessionaire), ballroom*
1934	Roof Garden Lounge*
1935	U-shaped pier*
1937	Dance pavilion*
1939	Roller-skating rink
1940	Grocery store, novelty and curio shop
1941	*Fairy Queen*, bowling alley (concessionaire), miniature golf (concessionaire)
1942	Miniature golf, shuffleboard courts
1944	Archery
1946	Ferris wheel, merry-go-round,* Roll-o-Plane (Bullet), Daddy Wahoo (concessionaire)
1949	Antique Auto Show
1955	Paradise Island*
1956	Terrainescope Observatory
1959	Ski show*
1961	*Shafer Queen* (wooden hulled)
1965	Dodg'em Cars,* Antique Auto Ride,* suspension bridge,* Skyroom Restaurant,* Skyride*
1967	Paratrooper ride*
1968	Go-cart track, Haunted House (concessionaire)

Year	Ride/Attraction
1969	*Shafer Queen*,* Mystery Mansion (Dark Ride, Den of Lost Thieves)*
1971	Galaxi,* Moon Bounce, Zugspitz
1972	Wabash Cannonball*
1976	Amusement gameroom*
1978	Spider, Superstition Mountain
1979	Flying Bobs*
1980	Paratrooper*
1983	Dr. Frankenstein's Haunted Castle*
1984	Tiger (Tig'rr)*
1986	Rocky Rapids Log Flume*
1987	Water park*
1989	Giant Gondola Wheel*
1990	Falling Star,* Boat Tag, Convoy Race
1992	Water swings*
1994	Hoosier Hurricane*
1995	Sky Coaster Thrill Ride*
1996	Fly High Parasailing (concessionaire)
1998	Big Flush Water Coaster,* Yogi Bear Jellystone Camp Resort (Ideal Park)
1999	Frog Hopper,* Double Shot*
2001	Cornball Express,* rock-climbing wall
2002	Lost Coaster of Superstition Mountain*
2004	Air Crow*
2005	Mini Pirate Ship*
2006	Splash Bash (Splash Battle)*
2007	Honey Creek Mining Operation,* motion picture theater
2008	Steel Hawg*
2011	Adventure Point*

*Rides/attractions still in use today

Chapter 5
THE SPACKMAN FAMILY

The Spackman family, who originally came from England, fought in the American Revolution, but at that time their name was spelled "Speakman." "They made munitions for George Washington," explained Joy Bailey, who traced the family history. Thomas Spackman was a private in a regiment in Pennsylvania. "They were indentured to Quakers, and later on they all became Quakers. During the time of the Revolution, they were not Quakers." Joy researched the family tree and is now a member of the Daughters of the American Revolution.

Earl William Spackman

Earl was born on August 3, 1875, in Lawrence, Pennsylvania, to Thomas and Matilda Spackman.

Earl enlisted in the U.S. Army on April 27, 1898, and served as a quartermaster during the Spanish-American War in 1898. He made it up to the rank of sergeant in Company K, First North Carolina Volunteer Infantry, in Mahaffey, Pennsylvania. He was honorably discharged on March 24, 1899.

He married Carolyn Bertha Stockman, who was born in London, Ontario, in 1905. In 1910, they lived in Greenfield, Michigan.

In 1918, the Spackmans lived on Coliseum Avenue in Indianapolis. Earl was a manager at the Henry Miller Foundry. Then he became a distributor for the Ideal Furnace Company in Indianapolis. Earl submitted a patent for an electric heater on March 23, 1925. The patent covered a portable heater as well as a fixed heater. His device used convection, whereas other heaters relied on conduction or radiation. His patent was approved on September 7, 1926. He sold the Ideal Heaters, which were made in Detroit at the headquarters for the Ideal Furnace Company.

With the backing of the furnace company, Earl's second occupation became the building of Ideal Beach in 1926. At first that venture didn't go very well, but bringing a dance hall to the resort turned it into a moneymaking venture for the entrepreneur. With Ideal Beach going so well for Earl, he decided to walk away from the Ideal

Earl Spackman founded Ideal Beach in 1926. *Courtesy Ruth Spackman Davis.*

Furnace Company in 1931, so he purchased a home in Monticello to be closer to his recreation area.

When he wasn't working, Earl played chess and became quite good at it. He once invited a world-famous chess player, George Koltawoski of Milwaukee, to Ideal Beach to play all comers. He taught his son Tom to play as well.

In 1945, Earl turned Ideal Beach operations over to his son, Tom.

On October 1, 1946, Earl suffered a heart attack and died while on vacation in Montreal, Quebec. Funeral services were held in Monticello. He was seventy.

After Earl died, Carolyn sold the park to Tom for a dollar. She remained as the dining room hostess. When the park closed for the winter, Carolyn would take the train out west and spend the winter in California. One of her sisters, Trude Gleason, would come to Monticello each year to visit with her.

Carolyn died on June 27, 1965. She had been ill for four years. She was buried in Mahaffey, Pennsylvania.

Thomas Earl Spackman (Sr.)

Thomas was born on July 5, 1913, in Highland Park, Michigan. Tom first worked at the concession stand at Ideal Beach when it opened. He was twelve years old at the time.

In 1933, Tom graduated from Shortridge High School in Indianapolis and decided to attend college to study business. This would give him the knowledge to follow in the footsteps of his father if he so desired.

Tom went to the University of California–Los Angeles for two years and then transferred to Indiana University, where he graduated with a bachelor's degree in business in 1937. He would later become a lifetime member of the Indiana University Emeritus Club. On July 13, 1937, he married Helen Quackenbush in Crown Point, Indiana. "He met her at a dance," explained his daughter, Joy.

In 1945, his father stepped aside, and Tom took over the park as the chief executive officer. After his father passed, Tom made major changes to the resort and turned it into more of an amusement park. Slowly, he added

Tom Spackman poses for a photo with Indiana Beach in the background. *Photo by Sue Erb.*

attractions as the budget permitted. This made Indiana Beach more exciting for those returning customers because there was always something new to see and do at the park.

While Tom managed the park, Helen cared for the three children they had at the time, as well as managing the dining room. Tom did teach his children how to swim. "He'd put an old belt around our waist and he would hold onto the belt," said Joy. "Then he'd say, 'Okay, now kick your legs and move your arms.' Then he'd let loose of the belt. We were supposed to be swimming, but it didn't quite work that way. I think we sank a number of times." They all did learn how to swim eventually though.

Tom would also take his children down the big wooden toboggan. He would swim right along with them. "He also liked to sail," added Joy. Her dad gave her a sailboat for her sixteenth birthday.

One of the things that Tom did every day was walk around the park to see if everything was going okay. He had a notebook to write down items that needed to be fixed. "He'd spend a couple of hours at his desk making phone calls," recalled his daughter Ruth Spackman Davis. "Most of the time, he would be out in the park and looking to see if things were running correctly." He had a system every night after the park closed to take his notes and put out orders to his people to fix the things that were wrong.

Tom built some of the cottages that were used at Indiana Beach by visitors. He got help from Harold Quackenbush, who was the foreman. "He and my dad argued, but they liked it," said Ruth. They never wrote anything down, but they knew where everything was located in the cottages.

Up until Paradise Island was built, Indiana Beach was more of a mom-and-pop operation. "Then it got bigger. They had to bring in more people to help," said Joy.

In May 1958, Tom joined with David Owen of Monticello to form Mattoon Lake Beach, Inc., which operated a summer resort at Mattoon Lake. They received a twenty-year lease to develop the sixty-five-acre property. Tom knew how to fly and used the plane to go to other resorts they owned in Effingham, Illinois, and Altoona, Iowa.

One of the things that Tom did was become friends with a lot of the bands and singers who came to Indiana Beach to perform. He sometimes brought them into his home to stay the night. Ruth recalled him bringing Tommy Sands to the house to stay. "I had to go to work, and I left him all alone," she said. "He must have thought that I was rude."

Later when the park got bigger, Tom took over care of the maintenance at the park because it was so important. "We have a term in the business: 'You do not want downtime,'" explained Ruth. "You keep your rides running. If something went down, he would quickly diagnose the problem."

One time, the *Shafer Queen* broke down and needed a part for the motor. "He sent a boy to New Orleans in a truck to pick it up and bring it back because you couldn't fly it or get it here anyway any quicker," Ruth explained. "In three days, we had it back up and going. He wanted to keep all the rides in good working order."

Tom had developed a whole list of people he could go to for each ride. "That was a big asset to have that all built up," Ruth said. Tom wasn't a mechanic, but he had developed a good understanding of how things worked. And if something needed to get done, Tom didn't mind rolling up his sleeves and taking care of the matter himself. Joe Seurynck, who has worked at Indiana Beach since 1971, recalled one time when Tom came walking down the boardwalk in his swimsuit and dove into the lake to recover an anchor that had fallen off the old *Shafer Queen*. Tom had to go down twice before he came up with the anchor.

Seurynck enjoyed working for Tom. There was a time when Joe got into a car accident and got injured. Tom told him, "You have a job when you get back on your feet." Tom did the same when Joe's wife delivered a baby. Tom treated his workers like they were family.

They also had some manufacturers they could call on for help, such as Chain Manufacturing. Generally, when they purchased a ride, they wanted the company to make repairs if that ride went down.

In the off-season, Tom and Carolyn would travel, and they loved going out west. Carolyn had a sister who lived in California, so she wanted to see her. She had ten other sisters and brothers in her family.

Tom also worked significantly to improve the industry's status and reputation locally, regionally, nationally and internationally. Locally, he helped promote the park as well as the city of Monticello. In fact, the Greater Monticello Chamber of Commerce presented him with its first Lifetime Achievement Award. The chamber also made him the first recipient of the George R. Armstrong Award. He created and funded the Visitor's and Lake Guide to promote Indiana Beach and the Monticello tourism industry. Tom was named as the winner of the State of Indiana "50 Year" Small Business Award in 1975.

Regionally, he turned Indiana Beach into a destination for many people in the state and the Midwest. In 1983, Tom took on additional responsibility as director of the Indiana Department of Tourism. He served in that position through 1989. Tom and Bill Koch of Holiday World had founded the predecessor to the state agency when they founded the Indiana Travel and Tourism Association. In 2003, Indiana governor Frank O'Bannon honored Tom with the Sagamore of the Wabash, the highest honor he could give to a business. The term "sagamore" was used by the Algonquin-speaking American Indian tribes of the northeastern United States for the tribal chiefs, while "Wabash" is a large river that flows in Indiana.

Tom and his wife, Helen, posed for this photo in 1991. The Giant Gondola Wheel is in the background. *Courtesy Ruth Spackman Davis.*

Locally, Tom always made an impact in the community by helping out many causes with free tickets or monetary donations or by serving on a board or committee. He was the co-chair with Dr. Nolan Hibner of the White County Memorial Hospital Capital Campaign that raised more than $900,000 for a new addition to the hospital. Tom served on the hospital board of directors for a long time.

Internationally, he was involved with International Association of Amusement Parks and Attractions (IAAPA) and served as its president once. The slogan "There's More Than Corn in Indiana" led to Tom receiving the promotion of the year from the IAAPA. Tom received the 2003 Meritorious Service Award from the IAAPA. Also, the State of Indiana Restaurant and Hospitality Association named Tom to its hall of fame in 2003.

Tom's hobby was playing chess like his father, and he became a championship player. He played against other champions around the world; they would send postcards to each other to show their next move. He sometimes played chess with patrons at the park. He was also an avid reader and enjoyed novels. He turned into a good dancer, as he personally enjoyed dancing to the big bands that played at the resort.

On July 7, 1993, two days after Tom's birthday and six days shy of their fifty-seventh wedding anniversary, Tom's beloved wife passed away.

Besides running the park, Tom was also involved in many charities, including the Give the Kids the World Campaign and Make-A-Wish Foundation. These programs give children special passes, and they are escorted around the park and given priority on any ride they are tall enough to get on.

In 2008, Tom entered an assisted living home to get better care. His children became his guardians.

Tom, who celebrated his 100th birthday on July 5, 2013, suffered a stroke in early November 2013. A week later, he passed away on November 11 at the White Oak Health Campus. His son Tom Jr. came back from Newbury Park, California, for the funeral. His other son, Jim, came from Cornville, Arizona. His daughters—Joy, Ruth and Cathy—lived in Monticello, so they had no travel involved. He left behind fourteen grandchildren and eleven great-grandchildren. Many were at the funeral, as well as more than one hundred other people, at his church, the Monticello Christian Church. In the casket, his family put a Hoosier Hurricane roller coaster pin and Indiana pin on his suit coat. In a drawer, they put keys, an arrowhead, a pen, an Indiana Beach card and Hershey kisses. Tom loved chocolate, although he never ate too much and remained slim throughout his life. They also left him with a notepad, as he used to walk the boardwalk and take notes. Finally, the family left him with a needlepoint that said "Back Home in Indiana," which was a slogan used in a commercial.

At the funeral, Bill Robinson gave the eulogy and spoke at length. The marketing agent had worked with Tom for a long time. One time at a meeting, they had discussed raising the price of admission to a dollar from fifty cents in order to pay for more marketing. "Tom said, 'Let's not get greedy,'" Robinson said. "He was a fair businessman," continued Robinson. "Nobody ever called to say they hadn't been paid."

Then Pastor Chris Dodson spoke about his parishioner of the last decade. He said Tom used to park his pickup truck in the church lot, and

Thomas Earl Spackman

Springer-Voorhis-Draper Funeral Home
Monticello, Indiana

The Spackman family came up with this logo to celebrate Tom's 100th birthday.

nobody would park near him because they feared him hitting them. His children eventually took the keys to the truck away from him. Tom once came to see the pastor on a Monday, requesting him to perform a wedding ceremony on Wednesday. Pastor Dodson asked him why, and he replied, "So I can get a car." Actually, he wanted to get married to a woman who had a car and could drive. His children had taken away his car keys because he had been in an accident and was getting too old to drive in his nineties.

Besides leaving behind a legacy, Tom left behind two sons and three daughters who all worked at Indiana Beach to make it a success, just as their father had done.

Thomas Earl Spackman (Jr.)

Thomas Earl Spackman (Jr.) was born on April 12, 1938, and given the same name as his father. His first recollection of the park was eating meals during the summer months in the original hotel dining room, where his grandmother was the manager.

Tom thinks he was about eight years old when he started working at Ideal Beach. He went around picking up empty Coca-Cola bottles in the parking lots. At that time, the bottles were six ounces and sold from a refreshment stand. They were also worth a monetary return. The cola was produced by the Monon Coca-Cola Bottling Plant.

He went to work at regular jobs at the park beginning when he was twelve. He worked for another ten years, while he was still in school, in many different jobs, including clerk in the skating rink, refreshment stand clerk and cook, soda fountain clerk, ride operator, reservation clerk, skating rink operator, dance hall manager, night office clerk, head of purchasing and various special assignments from his father. Tom saw a lot of bands when he was the dance hall manager. His favorite band was Boots Randolph.

All the Toms—Tom Jr., his father Tom and grandfather Tom—got together for a family portrait in 2002 at Ryan Spackman's wedding. *Courtesy Ruth Spackman Davis.*

Tom graduated from Monticello High School in 1956 and went on to Indiana University like his father. He graduated from IU School of Business in 1960 with a bachelor's degree in finance.

While attending IU, he met Carol Bridges, and they married in 1960. She went on to become a medical doctor. They have two children, Thomas Jr. and Linda. Linda worked for two years at Indiana Beach and Thomas for one year.

Instead of returning to Indiana Beach to work for his father, Tom started his career with General Electric in 1960 and held various management positions in the Information Systems Divisions of GE, Honeywell, Honeywell Bull and Bull HN Information Systems for thirty-six years. He lived in either Kentucky or Arizona during this time.

Tom returned to Indiana Beach in 1996 to become the general manager, replacing his aging father. When both Toms were working at Indiana Beach, they used Sr. and Jr. in press releases so that people wouldn't get them mixed up. He held that job until the Spackmans sold the park. He stayed around another two years as a consultant to help out the new owner. Then he moved to California in November 2011 to be close to his daughter and granddaughters, who live close by. His daughter, Linda, is married to Darryl Heller, and they have two daughters, Lauren and Julia. Their son also lives in nearby Arizona. Tom and his wife, Carol, enjoy the mild California weather compared to the four seasons of Indiana.

Now in retirement, Tom can enjoy his hobbies more. He likes to golf and play duplicate bridge. He also supports his granddaughters' activities.

James William Spackman

James was born on October 3, 1939. Like his brother before him, his first job at Ideal Beach was picking up bottles in the parking lot. Then he remembers working in the candy and candle store, refreshment stand, skating rink and wherever needed.

Jim also recalls a lot of things he did when he was young. He got into some mischief. One time when he was twelve, he was with his cousin Jim Quackenbush and his brother, Tom, and they bought some cigarettes from the cigarette machine. They also got some cigars and smoked everything by a fountain near the merry-go-round. When it was suppertime, they chewed on some gum to hide the smell and went home for dinner. "Harold

[Quackenbush] came running in and said that the dumpster was on fire," he said. His parents never found out their kids were responsible.

Jim, as he likes to be called, graduated from Monticello High School in 1957 and went on to get a business administration degree from Indiana University, graduating in 1962. Right after graduation, he married Sally Dinstin. "I met her at the park," he said. "She lived in Bloomington," where Jim went to college.

After they married, he continued to work at Indiana Beach and joined the U.S. Army National Guard in Monticello. Jim spent four years in the guard, and his unit was almost called up during the Vietnam War. He was in artillery.

Jim wore many hats while working at Indiana Beach for the next two decades. He helped with the design and construction of the Mystery Mansion (aka Dark Ride), master planning of the park, promotions, hiring and band scheduling, which he seemed to enjoy the most. He was able to land groups like the Beach Boys, Sonny and Cher and many others. "We'd space them out about every three weeks," he explained. They played on Friday nights because the ballroom would always have a crowd on Saturday regardless of who was playing.

Jim recalled one group that he booked for the Roof Garden Lounge. They were called the Big Thing and were all from DePaul University in Chicago. They played the latest Top 40 hits and were very good. They ended up becoming the group we all know now as Chicago. So some bands got their start playing at Indiana Beach.

Indiana Beach would advertise the concerts in the newspapers and on WLS radio in Chicago. "WLS was a good advertising draw," Jim said. Some fans followed the groups, so they would get fans from all over the country coming to Indiana Beach to see them play.

Some bands played too loud, and he asked them to leave. "We had a clause in their contract," explained Jim. "If they played too loud, we could cancel their contract."

While he was working at the park, Sally delivered two babies: James Ryan on October 5, 1971, and Ashley Paige on September 29, 1977. Neither of his children worked at Indiana Beach. Instead, they went on to other endeavors. Ryan graduated from Brown and Harvard University to earn a doctorate degree. He's now working for Noah Laboratory in Boulder, Colorado, as an atmospheric scientist. Ryan married, and now Jim has a grandson by the name of Abel Spackman as a result. Paige graduated from the University of Arizona and Wheaton College in Chicago, majoring in music. She's now in charge of sales for a plumbing company in Hampton, Virginia.

Tom, James Ryan and Jim Spackman had this photo taken in 2002 during Ryan's wedding. *Courtesy Ruth Spackman Davis.*

In the 1980s, Jim decided to leave Indiana Beach to go out on his own. The entrepreneur opened a clothing store in Tucson, but he found out that men don't really like to shop, so he got into real estate accounting until he landed a job as a business administrator for a large church. That was where he found his success, and he continued in that line of work until he retired.

His first wife, Sally, died of a heart attack on March 15, 1998. After she died, he returned to Monticello. "I came back after things started falling apart. The marketing plan wasn't working well," he explained. "They were trying to go after markets not really identified."

Jim said his father didn't like all the changes and the hassle the government provided with all its regulations and requirements, like taxes, building permits and the like. That led to his father wanting to sell the park in 2001. Another problem was coming up with something different every year. "You have to have some improvements every year," Jim said. This would keep people coming back to see what was new at the park.

In 2013, Jim married a woman he met online while living in Florida. He met up with Patricia Rohacs in Colorado, and they got married. Now they live in Cornville, Arizona, where Jim enjoys retirement. After five marriages, he said he's done with doing that again.

Jim turned out to be a chess player like his father and grandfather. He also enjoys watercolor painting and investing.

Joy A. (Spackman) Boomershine Bailey

Joy was born on June 9, 1941. She joined her brothers in picking up bottles in the parking lots at Indiana Beach when she was about ten years old. A few years later, she worked as a coat check in the ballroom. "I remember Louis Armstrong and all of the great bands," she explained. "I was able to listen to them and watch the people dance while I checked their hats and coats." Later on, she watched other acts, including the Smothers Brothers, the Kingston Trio, Sonny and Cher and Brenda Lee. She also worked in the soda stand, the hotel restaurant and anywhere else she was needed.

When the ski show began, she was in the first show. "Cypress Gardens came up and showed us how to ski and do the tricks," Joy said. "I didn't know how to water ski until they came." Joy was sixteen at the time.

She graduated from Monticello High School in 1959. She went on to Indiana University and marched in the band the first year. She was one of the Hoosierettes, now called Red Steppers. She twirled flags, marched and did some other things. Then she focused on her studies and graduated with a bachelor's degree in history. "I couldn't do anything with a degree in history," she said. So she went on to get a master's degree in teaching in 1965 at Indiana University–Kokomo. She also received a gifted-and-talented endorsement from Purdue University later on. While in school, she got a phone call from the superintendent at Monticello for a teaching job there. At first, she taught at the old Idaville High School for half days. The other half days she spent teaching preschoolers at the Presbyterian church. "Then I went and taught at Meadowlawn [Elementary]," she said. "I ended up teaching art." She taught art for twenty-six years at Twin Lakes School Corporation. "I loved teaching sixth grade." She also taught some other areas and retired from teaching after thirty-three years in 2000.

During much of this time, she worked at Indiana Beach during the summers. "Not every summer," she added. "After my children were grown, I could work at the beach." She worked in the gift stores.

Joy married Charles Garry Boomershine, who was also in the first ski show with her, although they didn't date until she was in college. They went on to have three boys: Bryan A., Daniel "Scott" and Christopher. Her sons all graduated from Indiana University and worked at Indiana Beach. Bryan now lives in Chicago; he's an artist and has an interior design store. Scott, an attorney, lives in Wilmette, Illinois. Chris lives in Indianapolis and is a captain with Homeland Security. He's also on a motorcycle drill team. "He really enjoys being in the parades," Joy said.

Her first husband died in 1982 from liver cancer at the age of forty-two. "Yeah, he was very young," Joy commented. "I had the three kids and managed to get them off to college."

In 1987, she married Richard Bailey. They are now both retired and live close to Indiana Beach. She likes to paint (watercolor and pastel), garden, read and play tennis.

"I guess we didn't realize at the time how different it was to grow up in an amusement park," Joy said. "It was really special. We didn't realize until later on in our lives how special that was."

Ruth Carol Spackman Davis

Ruth was born on January 12, 1945, in Lafayette, Indiana. She doesn't remember too much of Indiana Beach until she was twelve because she spent most of her early summers with babysitters; her grandmother would come to Monticello to care for her and Cathy or she would go to her grandparents' home in Bedford, Indiana. The other children were old enough to work at the park.

She was fourteen before she worked at Indiana Beach. She became a hatcheck girl in the ballroom when dances were being held there. "Which was a good experience, because I got to hear the big-name bands and I got to see the ladies come in and change into their formal attire," Ruth commented. "I got the tail end of the big band era." She particularly remembers Louis Armstrong and Glenn Miller's Orchestra. She has a copy of Miller's contract.

At age sixteen, she began working as a waitress in the restaurant in the Beach House Hotel before the Skyroom opened for business. At first she waited on the college students who lived in the hotel and worked at the resort. Then she moved up to waitress for regular customers. "That was a women's job," she added. "There were limitations on your opportunities."

Ruth graduated from Monticello High School in 1963, the last year for that school. Then she went on to Indiana University in Bloomington like the

The Spackmans pose for a family photo on the seventy-fifth anniversary of Indiana Beach. In the photo are (from left) Joy A. (Spackman) Boomershine Bailey, Ruth Spackman Davis, Tom Spackman Sr., Cathy (Spackman Juntgen) and Tom Spackman Jr. In the back row are mascots Rocky Raccoon, I.B. Crow and Yogi Bear. *Courtesy Ruth Spackman Davis.*

rest of the family. "I always came back in the summer and worked," she said. "That was a given. It wasn't a matter of working; it was a matter of where are you going to work."

She majored in social studies with some education classes. She remembers her father driving her down to IU the first year, as her mother didn't drive and she didn't have a car. "In my junior year, I got a car. You have to work for that car," Ruth said with a chuckle. Her first car was a Ford Mustang, a new car on the market at that time.

She graduated from IU in 1967. "My dad had made a deal with me," she explained. "It was the same deal with all of his kids. If we could get through college—the girls—without getting married, then he would send us on a trip to Europe." She went to Europe with a secretary from the park in the fall after the park closed for the summer. Her father didn't want to send her by herself, so he went along for the first two weeks of the trip. He got them a Eurorail pass for them to finish their vacation and went back home. They stayed another month traveling around Europe by themselves. "It was good, good memories. After you have children, you don't take trips like that for a while."

After she graduated, she moved to another job at the resort, working with her mother. "I started working in the clothing store, and I would go along with her on buying trips," Ruth said. She went to New York City once, but mostly they traveled to Chicago, Florida or the shows in Las Vegas. "There were a lot of salesmen who would visit us too. Once you pick up the hat, the hat stays on."

When her brother Jim left the park to pursue other entrepreneurial opportunities, she started doing the hiring for the park. "Most of the time, it was amazing. You have to have new help every year, but we were very fortunate that we had a core group. Like 80 percent of our people would come back. What you were replacing were the people who graduated from high school or went to college and didn't need a job anymore," Ruth explained. Her brother Jim had established the procedures, so she said it was "pretty easy to pick up."

One of the people she eventually hired was James Davis. A couple months later, she was dating him, and eventually she married him. Jim attended Indiana University and was in the Reserve Officer Training Corps. After he graduated, he was in the regular U.S. Army for four years. After his active duty stint, he joined the U.S. Army Reserve and later the U.S. Army National Guard. He retired as a colonel. Ruth and Jim went on to have three children: Tommy James, Ginny and Andrew. Tommy still works at Indiana Beach, while Ginny got married and now teaches at nearby Roosevelt Middle School in Monticello. Andrew is also married and works at the Monticello Post Office. All of them worked at Indiana Beach as youngsters. Jim also worked at Indiana Beach and had a concession as well. His last job was as vice-president.

Jim recalls when Debbie Knox from WISH-TV in Indianapolis came up to do a story on Indiana Beach. He took her on the Skyride, but it broke down. "Luckily, it broke down by the ski show," Jim explained. "I lied. I told her that I had them stop it so we could watch the ski show."

Later, when the park got larger, Ruth took on making up the schedule for the workers and taking care of maintenance. Ruth became the operations manager. To give her more time, she had to cut back on some of her store duties. She even went up to the Skyroom to help out occasionally because she could handle all the positions there. She would often hostess. "The end of the year was always hard because the kids would go back to school," she explained. "That's when foreign students became an asset. Their school didn't start until after Labor Day." She started hiring foreigners in the 1980s. "They liked working the extra hours."

The program allowed Ruth to hire a group of workers from a foreign nation and for that nation to hire Americans. It turned into a foreign exchange program that still exists today at the park. The foreign workers came to America on student work visas. The park had a car that the foreign students could use if they had an international driver's license.

"We made a lot of good friends with the international students," Ruth said. They still keep in touch with them today. "One of the international students married a local girl, and they are living here now, so he didn't go back. He liked it so much he stayed here."

Over her many years of working at the park, she has hundreds of good stories to tell. "When you work with the public, every day is a new day," she said. She got a kick out of the funny stories, and there was one every day. One of the funniest she recalled was when people would come in and ask, "Can you tell me how to get to Tu-ley-do?" They were asking how to get to Toledo, Ohio.

As far as singing groups, she loved Jim and Linda Bennett, who played the Skyroom. "They became a special draw. People came just for the entertainment," she said. She also liked the Dick Halleman Orchestra, which was a house band that played in the 1960s. They even played live music for the dance contests held there. "We danced every night," she said. The Eddy Howard Orchestra was another regular she recalled. "All of these groups became friends with Mom and Dad."

When the park was sold, Ruth was let go, although she made herself available to work. In fact, many of the veterans were let go. Today, the Davis family lives near the main entrance to Indiana Beach on Untalulti Drive. They have more time for their hobbies: reading, traveling and playing bridge.

Many employees worked at the park for many decades because the Spackmans treated them more like family than employees. For example, there was a time when former employee Eileen Wiltfong's car wouldn't start. So she called work and explained how she couldn't get to work. Jim came to her house to work on her car so she could come to work. When Eileen asked him why he came out, he responded, "You're part of the family." She worked there for sixteen years until the new company came in and didn't need her services as the bookkeeper. She was responsible for putting the accounting system on the computer.

During the time of the Spackmans, Indiana Beach also made several employees either full-time workers or salaried workers so they could get medical benefits and they wouldn't lose those workers over the off-season. For example, Bill VanDeman needed medical benefits because his wife couldn't get them, so he was made full time and his pay was spread out throughout the year. Finally, they made him a salaried worker.

Cathy Jo (Spackman) Juntgen

Cathy was born on March 26, 1951, and was the last child of Thomas and Helen Spackman. While she was growing up, she worked at the park. Her most interesting job was being on the ski team, which is where she skied alongside her future husband, Steven Juntgen. "Cathy was a gutsy skier," said Steve. She was also very good and skied for several years before the two married on July 18, 1970.

After they wed, the couple left Monticello, as Steve got a job with Bell Telephone in Naperville, Illinois. Then he went to work for Magnavox.

Meanwhile, Cathy became a mother when Michael D. was born on October 4, 1976. Then she had David on December 15, 1979. Her final delivery came on January 10, 1986, when she had Wendy. She focused on being a mother, while Steve focused on being a worker. Then the couple decided to purchase a franchise and got into the lawn care business in Fort Wayne. They did that for quite a while before selling it when the competition became too fierce as many others got into that type of business.

After they sold the business, Cathy's father, Tom, talked them into buying a Yogi Bear Jellystone Camp Resort franchise and opening it up by Indiana Beach to give the park more campgrounds. Steve said it was a $1.3 million investment. The business didn't do very well the first year, and Tom took over ownership. He then hired Cathy to run it for a year. When Tom refused to pay her full time through the winter months, she went back to Fort Wayne to work. After a year of absence, Cathy came back to run Yogi Bear Jellystone Camp Resort.

Tom put Steve in charge of the other Indiana Beach Campground. Steve found that campground to be in a mess, so he went about cleaning it up. "I redid the map of the campground," he said.

Steve said Tom was a good businessman. "He was a smart man. I learned so many things from him," Steve admitted. "He could take a problem and take care of it, but he wouldn't let it eat him up inside."

Cathy was the general manager of the Yogi Bear Jellystone Camp Resort until May 2013, when she decided to call it quits. She now works at the IU Health White Memorial Hospital.

Cathy, who was unable to be interviewed for this book, told the *Lafayette Journal Courier*, "It would be very sad to see what my dad built all of a sudden close."

Chapter 6
CONCESSIONAIRES

Earl Spackman began bringing in concessionaires in 1930. Some of them provided rides or attractions, while others brought food. Whatever Earl brought in, he got a piece of the profit to help make him more money.

One of the first concessionaires to bring in an attraction was Hugo Butler in 1941 with a miniature golf course. He also brought in other amusement rides, a speedboat and a large boat to drive people around the lake hourly. William Burbage of Monon operated a car ride and the miniature Monon train. Murl Hibbs of Monticello had a stand that sold popcorn, caramel crisp and taffy. Buck Wellman and Leslie Myers provided boats and marine supplies. Don Brown of Monon ran a French fry and fish sandwich stand. Dave Owens had an arcade. William Kreutzburg had an orange drink and frozen custard stand. Bob Sangster operated a moto-scoot track that was blacktopped, twelve bicycles and six outboard motor boats. Other concessionaires in the early days included Harold Barr and Fred Etchison.

Even some of the Spackmans invested in concessions and ran them. Joy Bailey's son ran a concession that was much like you see at carnivals. People would throw balls to knock over "cats" and win a prize. Jim Davis had concessions too.

By Indiana Beach's thirtieth anniversary in 1956, the park had more than fifty concessions. Tom Spackman required a minimum capital investment with bank references for people to be considered for a concession. He guaranteed 10 percent net return per year. He wanted concessionaires to be successful in order to keep their businesses there.

Tim and Carmin Eisele have owned the Pronto Pup stand for many years. *Photo by author.*

The oldest concession stand still remaining at the park is the Pronto Pup. Joe Skelton began the stand in 1947 when the park was still Ideal Beach. The stand was later sold to Bud and Nanna Eisele. Bud worked in the maintenance department, while Nanna ran the hot dog stand. When they decided to retire, the stand was passed down to their son, Tim. Nowadays, Tim and his wife, Carmin, run it and employ a dozen teens to work the stand. "This is a unique stand because you can see any of the food being prepared," Tim said. "Employees make the big difference. They're the face of the company." Tim also uses fresh oil every day to create his signature corn dogs that are called Pronto Pups. They come in regular size or foot long.

In 1954, Paul Ward saw the need for a store selling swimsuits at Indiana Beach and talked Tom Spackman into it. The store was called Kings Beachwear. It became the top seller of Jantzen swimsuits in the state. Ward ran the store for almost a decade until he sold it to the Spackmans. The store existed until a few years ago, when the new owners decided to close it down.

Another family that has been at the park for a long time is the Luchtman family, who have been at Indiana Beach for more than six decades. Jack and

Joan Luchtman began as a concessionaire in 1960 with a stand that served root beer, lemonade, orange slush and soft ice cream. It was located where the Skee Ball venue is today.

Then three years later, they purchased the cotton candy, sno-cone and roasted peanut concession from Miller's Concession. In 1974, the Luchtmans added the Nutty Banana, selling chocolate-covered bananas. They later added soft pretzels and colossal cones with hard hand-dipped ice cream.

Through the years, they added more concessions. "Joan and I had twenty-one stands at one time," Jack said. Helping to run them were his son, John, and daughter, Jill. Then Jill's son, Aaron Sims, grew up and helped out as well. In 2000, Jill took over the operation and has run it since.

The family built the Tiger's Den Restaurant and renovated the former Boardwalk Grill into the Beach Club, which was run by Aaron.

Nowadays, Jill (Luchtman) Speckman is running the many concessions at Indiana Beach, which include a Fudge Shop, Lake Shafer Princess, the Tiger's Den (a Dog 'n Suds franchise), a hot dog and drink stand, an ice cream and yogurt stand with more than twenty flavors and some other stands.

The Elephant Ears concession stand first came to Indiana Beach in 1975. The stand was built by Marvin and Alice Johns. It was doing really good business

Marvin Johns works on a sign at his elephant ears stand. *Photo by author.*

until September 11, 2001, the day America came under attack by terrorists. Johns said business dropped about 30 percent and has never recovered.

Johns liked the park more when the Spackmans owned it. He misses Family Day. The Spackmans made Thursday Family Day, and employees could bring in five people for free. "It was getting people out here," said Marvin. "The worst day turned into the best day."

The Taco Shoppe has been at Indiana Beach for twenty-eight years. Don and Sherry Long opened the stand, and now it is owned by their son, Greg Johnson. He took it over nine years ago.

The stand was featured on the Food Network several years ago and has been seen in reruns ever since. "It was beneficial to all at the beach," said the owner. An Alaskan couple saw the stand on television, and when they came to Indiana, they made it a point to visit the stand. "We have people come from Terre Haute and Cincinnati just for the tacos," said Greg. He advertises his place with a sign that says "World's Best Taco." He does a tremendous amount of business at the stand and from boaters who pull up to a nearby dock for his tacos. "They come from everywhere

People come from all over to eat the tacos at the famous Taco Shoppe, as it's been on television. *Photo by author.*

to go there," confirmed ticket salesman Ted Van Rijk. "Some come to the beach just to eat tacos."

One person complained about the stand running out of tacos a couple years back, but Greg said that was probably after the stand closed because he always has meat up until closing. Seven years ago, he opened a smoothie stand that does well, especially when the weather gets hot. He employs about twenty students during the summer and sells more than 100,000 tacos.

The Dippin' Dots concession began at Indiana Beach in 1994 and is operated by Bill and Mary Lou Metzger.

One of the newest concession stands is the Cliffhanger, which began operation under new owners John and Linda Komacko in 2012. They hired Jennifer Ousley to run the stand and another at Indiana Beach, as well as one in the campgrounds called Triple J Café. Jennifer had owned the Cliffhanger for five years prior to selling it to the Komackos. "It's a good business," she said. The two stands inside the amusement park offer lemon shake-ups and funnel cakes. The Triple J Café offers coffee, donuts, biscuits and gravy, ice cream and other treats. The Komackos employ about twenty people during the season.

Over the years, there have been many concessionaires, and some have been there for decades, like Wilma and Jim Miller. They owned and operated Miller's Concession for forty years.

Chapter 7

HAUNTED INDIANA BEACH

Since Indiana Beach has been around since 1926, it only seems natural that those who enjoyed the park would want to remain in spirit. Some say they still haunt the park today.

On a cool evening in August 2013, the Lost Limbs Foundation held a paranormal convention in Monticello, and one of the events was a visit to Indiana Beach to do a paranormal investigation with SyFy Channel celebrity Steve Gonzales from the hit TV show *Ghost Hunters* and local ghost writer Dorothy Salvo Davis. They led more than one hundred VIP ticket holders in the investigation. All the ghost hunters met in the old, rundown ballroom where orchestras played big band music and rock-and-roll groups shook the house. Some people have said they have seen a couple doing an elegant waltz in the ballroom, and they believed the couple was none other than the founders of the beach, Earl and Helen Spackman. That evening, no one caught a glimpse of the couple, but recorders captured some old music of yesteryear. There was no music playing in the park, as it was closed for the night.

The large group broke down into smaller groups to investigate different areas. One group went to Dr. Frankenstein's Haunted Castle to investigate the feeling of heat some get there or the smell of smoke. Near the castle was once the old Haunted House that burned down in 1980. One man got a ghost recording, called an electronic voice phenomenon, just outside the castle with a woman's voice saying, "It is gone. It is gone!"

Then Steve and his group went to a cabin that belonged to maintenance man Harold Quackenbush. When he was in the cabin, an odd knocking came from the basement. They went to investigate but found nothing. Other maintenance workers claim they have seen Quackenbush watching over them. He's a friendly spirit and has even said "Hello" to them before disappearing.

Steve enjoyed his trip to Indiana Beach. "Parks like this you don't see anymore," he said. "I think it is great just seeing it is still going."

On the evening of the celebrity investigation, there was some unexplained evidence. The park itself is a wonderful place of nostalgia.

Chapter 8

REVIEWS

Reviews about Indiana Beach in recent times have ranged from "great" down to "terrible," but generally they are favorable.

The Indiana Beach Facebook page gives it a rating of four and a half stars out of five.

Theme Park Review has reviewed amusement parks all over the world and at the end of 2013 gave Indiana Beach a three-and-a-half-star rating, while its members gave it four stars out of five.

Yahoo Travel gave the park a three-out-of-five rating. Reviews ranged from "First time is the last time" to "Great place to be to ease your troubled mind" and "Can't wait to take the kids back."

Trip Advisor gave Indiana Beach a two and a half out of five rating based on 212 reviews over the last few years. The hotel there only got a two out of five rating; however, it was built in the 1950s. Reviews ranged from "Indiana Beach is a waste of money" to "Good place for people of all ages" and "Still good old fashioned fun."

Yelp gave Indiana Beach a three-out-of-five rating based on eight reviews.

Perhaps one of the reviewers summed it up best when they said, "I think many of the other reviewers missed the point. This is NOT Cedar Point, and it's not the Hilton. It's a small, old, historic, and unique amusement park that should be enjoyed as a piece of Americana."

BIBLIOGRAPHY

Across Indiana, WFYI Television
Kokomo Tribune
Lafayette Journal Courier
Logansport Pharos-Tribune
Monticello Evening Journal
Monticello Herald
Monticello Herald Journal
WLFI Television
www.Facebook.com/AlanJenkins
www.imdb.com
www.IndianaBeach.com
www.themeparkreview.com
www.travel.yahoo.com
www.tripadvisor.com
www.Wikipedia.com
www.Yelp.com

INDEX

Index

C

D

ABOUT THE AUTHOR

Indiana Beach is W.C. Madden's fourth title with The History Press. He has written thirty-five books, hundreds of magazine articles and thousands of newspaper/newsletter articles during his thirty-eight-year writing career.

He began writing in 1976 as a reporter for a weekly newspaper in the United States Air Force. His writing abilities led to his becoming an editor in 1977 and winning numerous writing awards, including the highest military journalism honor, the Thomas Jefferson Award, for having the best newspaper in its category in the military. Then he taught journalism in the military for three years. He also taught for four more years after retiring from the U.S. Air Force, including a year at Indiana University/Purdue University at Indianapolis.

Madden broke into magazine, writing as a freelance writer in 1984 for the *Indiana Business Magazine*. He wrote numerous articles for the magazine over a three-year period. He also broke into the national market with some articles in *Entrepreneur Magazine*.

After retiring from the U.S. Air Force in 1986, he edited a civilian newspaper for three years while completing a journalism degree with Our Lady of the Lake University in San Antonio, Texas. He became a technical writer and worked six years for two different companies. In 1994, Madden began writing books on a regular basis.

When not writing, he volunteers his time to the Monticello Christian Church and the Literacy Volunteers of White County. Madden is a lifetime member of the White County Historical Society.

He currently publishes a quarterly magazine, *Monticello Magazine*.

Visit us at
www.historypress.net

....

This title is also available as an e-book